Saints of the Byzantine World

Saints of the Byzantine World

BY BLANCHE JENNINGS THOMPSON

illustrated by Donald Bolognese

VISION BOOKS

FARRAR, STRAUS & CUDAHY — NEW YORK

BURNS & OATES — LONDON

Nihil Obstat:
Rt. Rev. Msgr. Peter B. O'Connor
Censor Librorum

Imprimatur:
✠ Most Reverend Thomas A. Boland, S.T.D.
Archbishop of Newark

The nihil obstat and imprimatur are official declarations that a book or pamphlet is free of doctrinal or moral error. No implication is contained therein that those who have granted the nihil obstat and imprimatur agree with the contents, opinions or statements expressed.

Vision Books
Is a Division of
Farrar, Straus & Cudahy, Inc.
Published Simultaneously in Canada by
Ambassador Books, Ltd.,
Toronto.
Manufactured in the U.S.A.

Contents

Author's Note

Since many of the names, dates, and events associated with the early Church are still a matter of debate among scholars, the material chosen for this book has been taken from some of the most commonly accepted sources. The great heresies and other conflicts of those times are necessarily reduced to simplest terms in order to place the emphasis upon the characters and lives of the saints.

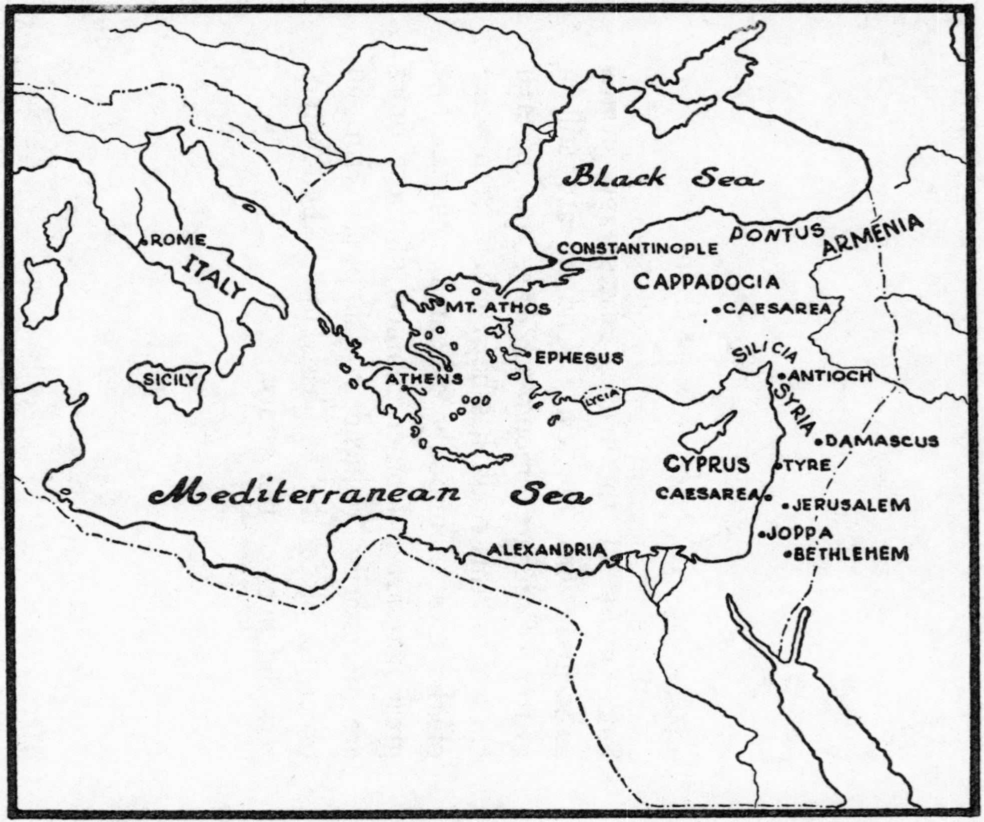
Black Sea
PONTUS
ARMENIA
CONSTANTINOPLE
CAPPADOCIA
CAESAREA
ROME
ITALY
MT. ATHOS
EPHESUS
SILICIA
ANTIOCH
SICILY
ATHENS
LYCIA
SYRIA
DAMASCUS
CYPRUS
TYRE
Mediterranean Sea
CAESAREA
JERUSALEM
JOPPA
ALEXANDRIA
BETHLEHEM

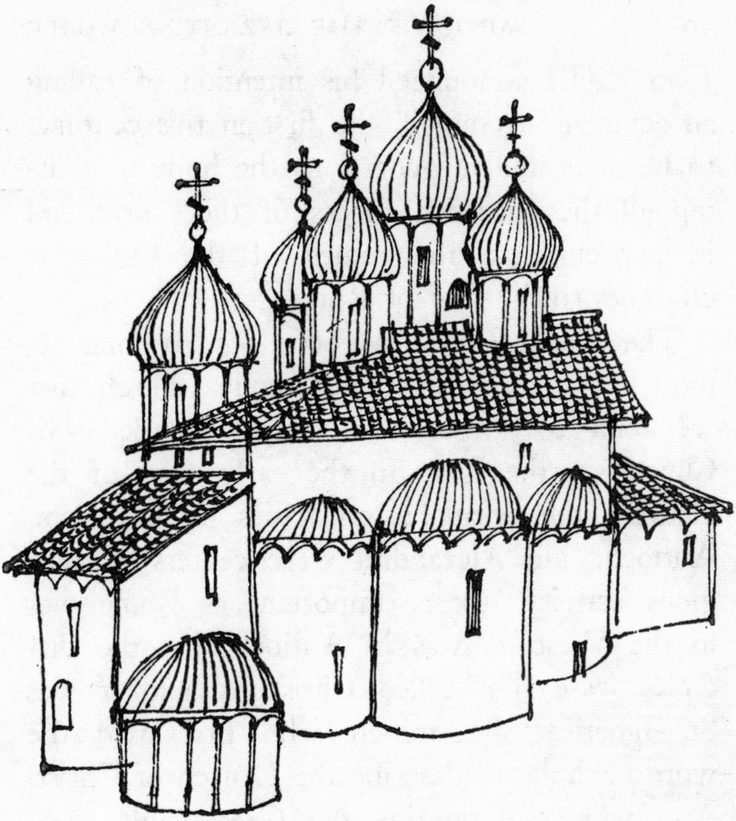

CHAPTER ONE

The Eastern Church

It was in the year 1054 that a large segment of the Eastern branch of the Catholic Church, after centuries of strife and misunderstanding, broke with the West completely and rejected the authority of the Pope. The breach has never been healed.

Not long after his coronation in 1958, Pope

John XXIII announced his intention of calling an ecumenical council, the first in this century, to be dedicated in general to the hope of uniting all the Christian forces of the world and in particular to the return of the Orthodox churches to the fold of Rome.

The word Rome has been for so long almost a synonym for the Catholic Church that we tend to forget that Christ founded His Church in the East. In the early days of the Church, the great Eastern cities of Jerusalem, Antioch, and Alexandria were centers of religious activity just as important as Rome was in the West. It was in Antioch that the disciples were first called Christians, and it was St. Ignatius of Antioch who first used the word Catholic to describe the Church of Christ. And when Constantine the Great built Constantinople on the site of ancient Byzantium, that fabulous city preserved the ideals of Christianity for centuries and was called by its citizens "the city guarded by God."

From the beginning, however, Eastern Christianity lacked unity. Each city was the center of a separate church, colorful, fiercely individual, and possessed of its own special liturgy. There was great rivalry among them, but they all believed in the same truths and remained members of the Universal Church under the

Bishop of Rome who eventually became known as the Pope.

During the fearful persecutions under the Roman rule, Eastern Christians hid in the deserts and mountains as those of the West did in the catacombs. When the pressure was finally lifted and the Christians were able to live and worship in comparative peace, many became lax and worldly. Others, fearing this trend, fled in thousands back to the Egyptian desert, this time to save their souls by living as anchorites or solitaries. Among the greatest were St. Paul the Hermit, St. Antony of Egypt, St. Hilarion, and St. Pachomius. These "desert fathers" founded the first monasteries and taught men how to serve God in community life.

In those first centuries not only persecution but heresy disrupted the Church. Men of power and influence preached false doctrines and misled the people. In the year 325, when the terrible Arian heresy was keeping the Eastern Churches in turmoil, Emperor Constantine, with the approval of Pope Sylvester, called what is generally regarded as the first ecumenical council for the purpose of defining the doctrines of the Church and correcting error. Then God raised up men of mighty stature: St. Athanasius, St. Basil the Great, St. Gregory Nazianzen, St. Gregory of Nyssa, and St. John

Chrysostom of the golden tongue. They defended God's holy word and suffered persecution and exile for His name.

As time went on, the Eastern and Western branches of the Catholic Church grew away from each other. They were separated not only by distance but by temperament and culture as well as language. The Western Church adopted Latin for its liturgy. The Eastern branch used chiefly Greek or national languages. There were, in addition, economical and political differences, to say nothing of the great conflicts caused by heresy. In 1054 occurred the final break known as the Eastern Schism, or separation. The millions who still cling to Rome but retain their own liturgies constitute the Church of Eastern or Oriental Rite, the largest group being those of the Greek, or Byzantine, Rite. Other millions, still separated, comprise the Orthodox churches. They use much the same liturgies as the Eastern Rite Catholics, but they still refuse to recognize the Pope as the vicar of Christ on earth.

The Eastern Church was rich in saints: St. Nicholas of Myra, the children's saint, and St. Simeon Stylites who took refuge from the world on top of a tall pillar. St. Cyril of Jerusalem and St. Cyril of Alexandria raised valiant tongues against heresy. St. Macrina, sister of St. Basil, was a leader of the holy women.

St. John Damascene battled the Iconoclasts; Sts. Cyril and Methodius were Apostles to the Slavs; and Sts. Antony and Theodosius founded the first monastery in Russia. All are honored in the liturgies of both West and East.

Those who read this book will surely come to love the Byzantine saints and will earnestly pray that their brothers of the Orthodox churches may soon return to the Mother Church of Rome.

As Pope Benedict XV said: "The Church of Jesus Christ is neither Latin nor Greek nor Slav, but Catholic; accordingly, she makes no difference between her children, and Greeks, Latins, Slavs, and members of all nations are equal in the eyes of the Apostolic See."

CHAPTER TWO

St. Antony of Egypt

And suddenly there came a sound from heaven, as of a violent wind blowing, and it filled the whole house where they were sitting.

In those early days of the Church there was a kind of holy excitement in the hearts of believers, something of spiritual splendor. After the dramatic and astounding descent of the Holy Spirit, the ensuing miracles, and the inspired preaching and example of the Apostles, the first Christians were, like Stephen, filled with grace and power. In the awful days of the persecutions they lived heroic lives, and thousands died as martyrs. Then came comparative peace and the reaction that often follows. Tempted by the pagan life around them, not a few Christians lost their former zeal and became weak in faith and worldly.

In the Eastern Church many of the faithful, seeing how easy it was to become lax in times of peace, feared for their souls' salvation. They began to withdraw from the world entirely and retired into desert places where they might think of nothing but God and serve Him with all their hearts. At first these men were called solitaries, anchorites, or hermits. Eventually they all became known as monks. The word monk comes from a Greek word meaning alone. By the beginning of the fourth century thousands of monks were to be found in the deserts of Egypt, Syria, Mesopotamia, and Palestine.

It was in Egypt, in the latter part of the third century, that the first of the anchorites appeared. At first they did not go far from home. They lived, each by himself, in caves or rude shelters and tried by penance, mortification, prayer, and labor to order their lives so that they would be pleasing to God. The very first one of whom there is any record is Paul the Hermit. He was a gentle, quiet, well-educated young man who, when he was about twenty-three years old, withdrew into the Egyptian desert, praying that God would show him what to do. He took nothing with him but his cloak and his staff and began to look for a suitable place to live.

The desert sand was loose and dazzling white, very difficult to wade through. It was studded with huge granite blocks, with not a bush, a blade of grass, or a patch of moss to be seen, but there were hills of limestone full of holes and caverns which had been used as dwellings in the pre-Christian era. Paul, exploring such a cavern, pulled away a great stone at the entrance. Inside was a wide space with a tall palm tree in the center making a shady roof, and in a hollow of the rock was a spring of clear water. This was the place for him, Paul thought. There was water, shelter, dates for food, and leaves for clothing—everything he needed. He lived there ninety years. When he was a hundred and thirteen years old, he knew that his end was near—but what happened then belongs to the story of another great and famous saint.

The first Christian monk whose name we know was St. Antony of Egypt. He was born of Christian parents in the year 251. It was a time of peace for the Church, but Christians were set apart from other people. They did not have full citizenship, and they always lived in the fear of another persecution. Nevertheless Antony was happy and contented in his home. He was a quiet child who never cared much for games and usually refused sweetmeats or delicate foods. He was educated at home by tutors and, like most Christians, learned the Scriptures by heart. Not only Christians, but everyone with an education in those days had this extraordinary ability to memorize whole books and scriptures. It was required in the schools. Books were scarce, and an educated man carried most of his library in his head.

Antony's parents died when he was about eighteen or twenty, and he became the guardian of his younger sister. One day in church he heard the priest read: "If thou wilt be perfect, sell all thou hast and give to the poor and follow me." Antony listened and believed. Part of the estate left by his parents consisted of three hundred acres of very productive land. He sold a large part of it and gave what he received to the poor. Shortly afterward he again heard the priest read a challenging message: "Be not solicitous for the morrow." This time Antony sold all that remained, placed his sister with a community of holy women, and moved to a cave not far from his home. There he led a simple, prayerful life.

Already there were a few anchorites in the

neighborhood, and Antony visited them in turn, noting all the best points of each one's way of living. He tried to practice fasting, prayer, and penance as they did to keep his mind off worldly affairs. The devil, naturally, did his best to make the young man discontented. He tempted him with fears about his sister, with the desire for rich foods, for money, fame, and companionship. It is hard to leave a comfortable home as Antony did and learn to live on bread and water with a little salt. He ate only once a day, after sunset, and took his sleep afterward on the bare ground.

For several years Antony lived in this manner. He learned to make mats and baskets out of palm leaves and bark and sold them to buy bread and salt. The people of the town liked him and often brought their problems to him because he was so cheerful, kind, and patient, and gave them such good advice. But the devil did *not* like him. He sent companies of demons to plague Antony. They often came in the shape of animals who battered him until morning light, but he continued to pray and defy them. One morning after he had had a particularly bad night, he saw a ray of light over the roof. Antony looked up and said to God somewhat reproachfully, "Where were you, Lord?"

"I was here, Antony," said the Lord, "waiting and watching your struggle. I will always be your helper, and I will make your name renowned throughout the world."

Antony didn't care for renown, and he probably didn't even realize what God's words meant. He decided that he would go farther into the desert. He was about thirty-five years old at this time, strong and handsome, showing no trace of his fasts and penances. Antony had great sweetness of spirit and a sort of grace or power that expressed itself in many miracles of healing. He was greatly loved by the people; still he felt that he should live in greater solitude. Far out into the desert he went, therefore, and found an old abandoned fortress with high walls. He took enough bread with him for six months and arranged with a friend to have a supply brought to him twice a year. For twenty years he lived in that fort seeing no one. Even the friend who brought the bread had to toss it over the wall. He was still greatly troubled by demons, but he endured them with patience and courage.

When Antony was about fifty-five years old, the people who wanted his help came and broke down the doors of the fort. They begged him to come out and be their guide and healer. When he did come out, very reluctantly, they were astonished to see that he had not changed at all in appearance. He always looked strong and kind and sensible and very reassuring. Although he did not really like to work miracles, he did so—but only at a distance. The people wanted the blessing of his touch but Antony said, "No, go back home and you will be cured." They went and they *were* cured, but they were not satisfied. They came in such numbers that they made a road to his tower. Finally he had to leave his fortress and come out to serve the people and especially the monks, hundreds of whom had made for themselves shelters of one kind or another in order that they might be near him. These new shelters were different from the older type. They were built in small groups at varying distances from each other, and they came to be called lauras.

Antony now began to instruct the monks and to give them some organization and a plan for living. Since the lauras soon spread out over considerable territory, he visited each one in turn, often crossing rivers infested with crocodiles and encountering other dangers. It was there in the Egyptian desert that the monastic life of the Church began. Those crude lauras were the forerunners of the monastery, and Antony was the first abbot.

The early monks were really amazing characters. In general, they were honest, humble, spiritual men, cheerful and happy, living contentedly in God's shadow and singing His praises night and day. They worked hard and silently, prayed and fasted, and tried to help the poor and the afflicted. Of course there were some among them who were misfits. In any great mass movement there are inevitably some who do not truly belong, and so it was with the first monks. The great majority of them, however, were remarkable men who lived good and holy lives.

In the beginning, each monk lived as a solitary or ascetic like Paul the Hermit. They visited one another and worked together to build their little cells of wood thatched with palm leaves. They wove mats and baskets and sold them to buy bread for themselves and for the poor. It might be wondered where they could sell the thousands of mats and baskets they must have made, but actually there was a ready market for them. All over the East mats are used for dozens of purposes, and since they wear out easily, replacements are constantly needed. Many of the baskets were carried by pilgrims.

Sometimes the monks helped neighboring farmers with the harvest. Some had small vegetable gardens to provide food for pilgrims and travelers. They themselves ate only bread and salt as a rule. Their rough shelters contained two stools and a sheepskin for a bed, a water jar, and sometimes a little oil or wine for strangers. We who require such a varied and tempting diet find it hard to believe that the monks could exist on so little, but they did—and they thrived on it. Many of the monks tamed wild animals for pets. They memorized the Scriptures and repeated psalms and prayers at intervals during the day, and on Sundays they went to the village church to hear Mass and receive the Sacraments. Whenever Antony arrived at one of the lauras, they gathered eagerly to listen to his sermons.

Antony was always a persuasive speaker. At one time while he was still living alone in his fortress, the emperor Maximian was persecuting the Christians most cruelly. Antony, who would have been very happy to die a martyr's death, left his tower and hastened to the arena in the city to console those who were condemned to die. Dressed in his white sheepskin tunic, he preached to the martyrs and gave them strength and courage, but he himself, to his disappointment, was not arrested or disturbed. He was banished from the city, however, and had to return sadly to his desert cell.

As he grew older, Antony longed to go back to the inner desert where he would have more time to pray and meditate. He asked for a pronged hoe, an ax, and some corn. Then far off in a quiet place he tilled a small piece of land near a shallow stream and planted a few vegetables for visitors. He made little ditches or canals to irrigate the dry soil. Then, when the corn was high, some wild horses came and ate it. Antony took one of them by the ears.

"Why do you eat what you have not sown?" he asked. "Why do you injure one who has not harmed you? Go, in the name of God!"

And the horses went.

When Antony was ninety years old, he believed that he was the oldest monk in the desert and that God must be well pleased with him, but God, lest Antony sin by pride, sent him a vision in which he learned of a solitary who was much older and holier than he. This man was Paul the Hermit, and Antony determined to visit him. It was a two-day journey across the desert, and Antony didn't know where to look until he saw a wolf go into the entrance to a cave. It turned out to be Paul's cave, but at first Paul would not let Antony enter. It took Antony two hours to talk Paul into letting him in, but when at length he did so, he seemed greatly pleased. He asked Antony for news of the world, who was emperor, and how Christianity was faring. Suddenly, a crow flew down and placed a loaf of bread before them. Paul was delighted.

"Look," said he, "God has sent us our dinner. God the merciful, God the compassionate. For sixty years now I have received a half loaf of bread every day, but at your coming God has doubled his soldier's rations." Then Paul and Antony argued politely as to who should break the loaf, Antony, who was the guest, or Paul, who was the elder. In the end they both took hold of the loaf and together broke it in two.

God must have looked down lovingly at the two dear, holy old men as they accepted the little extra ration so gratefully, hoping to strengthen their bodies and serve Him another day, should that be His will.

As Antony was leaving, Paul said to him, "My brother Antony, God promised me that I should see you before I die. He has sent you to me so that you may cover my body with earth. How good God is to me!"

"Oh, take me with you," said Antony.

"No, wait patiently. Your example is still necessary to the other monks. But bury me like a dutiful son. Go now and bring the cloak that Bishop Athanasius gave you and cover me with it for my burial."

Antony was astonished that Paul knew about the cloak. He started out immediately to get it, not knowing that Paul had used the cloak as an excuse. He knew that he was about to die, and he wanted to spare Antony's feelings.

While he was returning with the cloak, Antony saw a host of angels bearing Paul's soul to heaven. When he reached the cave he found Paul kneeling upright under a palm tree. Antony wept as he covered the good old man with the cloak and said the prayers of Christian burial. Afterwards, he began to wonder how he would be able to dig the grave, but two large lions came to him quietly, licked his hands as if they were pet dogs, and proceeded to dig it for him. Then they withdrew as silently as they had come while Antony blessed them with psalms of praise. He took Paul's penitential garment of woven palm leaves with him in exchange for the cloak of Athanasius and always wore it at Easter and Pentecost.

In his very old age Antony saw his sister again. She had become the superior of that little group of holy women with whom he had left her as a child and which had become the first known convent. For the last fifteen years he lived in the inner desert with two young monks close at hand. They had promised that when he died they would bury him in a secret place and tell no man where they had laid him. They kept their promise.

Antony lived to the age of 105. During his lifetime he knew many famous people. Even the Emperor Constantine sent a humble request for Antony's advice and prayers. The great St. Augustine tells in his *Confessions* that he was converted by hearing of Antony and his teachings. No one knows how many souls he saved, but he is remembered chiefly as the father of monastic life and as one of the chief defenders of the Church against the Arian heresy. Because of his power over animals he is known as the patron saint of herdsmen, and, no doubt, in his humility, that is the honor that would have pleased him most.

CHAPTER THREE

St. Hilarion

Hilarion was the name they gave him. When he was born near Gaza in Palestine, his pagan parents rejoiced because the stars were favorable and would bring good fortune to their son. The third century was near its close. St. Paul the Hermit was dwelling quietly in his rocky cave, and not far away St. Antony of Egypt was living as a solitary. The stars were indeed favorable for the pagan boy.

Hilarion grew up gentle and delicate, and obviously had a brilliant mind. Since the family was wealthy, his parents wanted him to have the best education possible. In those days a boy was sent to school at about the age of five. He was usually sent to the home of his tutor in charge of a servant called a pedagogue, not infrequently a slave, who carried his master's books, took care of him in general, and disciplined him when necessary. If the boy could not answer the assigned questions, the tutor nodded to the pedagogue who gave his master a good sharp switch with a long rod or ruler. That usually speeded up the learning process. The boys studied reading, writing, and spelling at first, and when they reached the age of ten, grammar was added. They memorized Aesop's fables, as well as long passages from Plato, Aristotle, and other classical writers. Later there was much emphasis upon rhetoric, exposition, argument, and debate. Hilarion was the joy of his tutors. No pedagogue ever had to touch him with a switch.

It was not long before Hilarion was ready for higher education, and he was sent to a famous school in Alexandria. Now Alexandria was in Egypt, and St. Antony was in Egypt. Hilarion heard about Antony's teaching and felt himself much attracted to such a way of life. He was not satisfied with the pagan philosophy that he had been absorbing. He seems also to have come in contact with some Christians at this time and was much impressed by their doctrine. He determined to seek out Antony in the desert and become his disciple.

Hilarion was not quite fifteen and still far from rugged, but he laid aside his worldly clothing, put on a tunic of rough cloth with an outer coat of sheepskin, and with a stout staff in his hand made his way to the desert. There he built a rude shelter like those used by the other anchorites. It was about this time that St. Antony was so beset by disciples and by people who wanted his advice that he had to leave his fortress shelter and come out to minister to them. Among the throng was a very new and very young disciple who studied Antony from a distance.

As the boy watched he was decidedly impressed and at the same time disappointed. He noted how gracious and humble Antony was and how patiently he answered questions and explained points of doctrine. He was repelled, however, by the crowds that closed in on Antony wherever he went and kept bothering him with their little problems or asking unimportant questions. Antony might just as well have stayed in town, thought Hilarion, if he were to be pushed and prodded by crowds like this. What was the use of trying to be an anchorite if there was to be no solitude, no peace, no time for prayer and penance?

The other anchorites surrounding Antony became very fond of Hilarion. They admired his gentleness and courage and believed that he was destined for great holiness. Antony himself felt that God had some special plan for the young anchorite. He agreed with him that it was best to begin as a solitary and to stay that way, too, if God so willed it. The important thing was to accept God's will. He gave the boy his blessing.

Hilarion returned to his own country, where he found that his parents had died and that a considerable inheritance was awaiting him. He divided part of it among his brothers and sisters, gave a large share to the poor, and, after giving away all his personal possessions, started out to be a true disciple of Christ and practice perfect poverty. All his relatives and friends tried to dissuade him. He was so young and frail that he touched the hearts of all who knew him, but there was nothing frail about Hilarion's will. He made a hair shirt for himself and a sheepskin cloak, and taking a few dried figs for food he started out on his journey.

Down to the seaport went the young Hilarion. The long marshy strip of coast stretched out all the way to Egypt and the mouth of the Nile. It was a dreary, desolate, swampy place, rough with reeds and rushes, infested by flies and gnats. Robbers and murderers used it as a hiding place and leaped out upon unwary travelers. They plundered caravans and escaped into the desert beyond. It was a rough and dangerous place for a boy not yet sixteen, but Hilarion was courageous and determined. Once well out in the desert he built himself a little hut of mud and turf. He thatched it with leaves and wove a mat of rushes as he had learned to do in the lauras of Egypt. He made up his mind that he would eat fifteen dried figs as his daily fare and that it would be best to eat that meal just after sundown. He had thought a good deal about the life of a solitary and had come to the conclusion that every monk should do some manual labor every day. He therefore made a little garden and grew a few vegetables, but he did not eat any of them.

Working with rushes was difficult for Hilarion. He found the stiff stems hard to handle, and the sharp edges cut his hands when he was weaving. Nevertheless he persisted. He was often tempted by memories of the world he had left and of the comforts to be found there. When this happened he was angry at himself and concluded that he should fast more strictly. He ate his allotted portion of figs only every third or fourth day and drank bitter juice made from marsh grass. It took a great deal of courage and will power, but he mastered himself and lived in this way, fasting, praying, and working, until he was about twenty years of age.

Although Hilarion's shelter was far from the traveled roads, he was not always alone by any means. Once some robbers tried to find his cell, not to rob him for there wasn't much to rob, but to frighten him. They wandered about all night but did not find the place until morning. Then they discovered him placidly weaving rushes into a mat and were surprised that he showed no fear. They pretended to be friendly.

"What would you do in this lonely place," said one, "if robbers or murderers should surprise you?"

"I would not fear them," said Hilarion. "I have nothing for robbers."

"But they might kill you in their anger if they found nothing."

"That would not matter. I am ready to die if God wills it," answered Hilarion, pulling his rushes tight.

The robbers were very much impressed. This was a new way of looking at things. They went on their journey talking it over and, according to the story, decided to change their way of life.

For twenty-two years Hilarion lived in his desert cell. He had taken with him a copy of the Scriptures which he had made himself as a young boy, and these he memorized and studied constantly. He sang psalms and hymns and spent much time in meditation. Of course people began to tell each other of the holy man out in the desert and, just as in the case of St. Antony, they began to go out to see him and ask for his help. He gave them wise advice and worked many miracles.

One famous miracle concerned the wife of the governor of Palestine who had taken her three sons to see St. Antony of Egypt. While they were staying at an inn on the way home, all three of the boys were suddenly stricken by fever. The frightened mother had the children taken home to Gaza, where the best physicians could not control the fever. A maid-servant told the mother about Hilarion. With the permission of her husband, who was desperate at his sons' illness, she went to Hilarion's cell and begged him to go back with her. He told her that he would not dream of going even to a small village, to say nothing of the city of Gaza, but she fell to her knees and implored him.

"For the love of our holy Lord Jesus, save my children," she begged. "Glorify His name and put the pagan idols to shame."

At last Hilarion promised that he would go, though most reluctantly. He reached Gaza at sunset and prayed at the bedside of the dying boys. Immediately the fever subsided, to the astonishment of the doctors and the joy of the governor and his wife. The whole household marveled when the boys opened their eyes and asked for something to eat.

Of course, after that incident, Hilarion's fame spread far and wide. He began to realize Antony's problem because now he, too, was obliged to give up his solitude. His cell became a place of pilgrimage. Unbelievers came to talk with him and went away convinced that the Christian faith was the only true teaching. Most disturbing of all, disciples began to gather around him and to congregate in lauras as they had done around Antony.

Hilarion gave up. Until that time there had been no monasteries or communities of monks in Syria or Palestine. Hilarion decided that he would have to organize his followers in some way as Antony had done. There were now both men and women among them, for the women wanted to work for eternal life, too, and they gathered in lauras of their own. Antony heard and approved and sent many sick and troubled persons to "my son Hilarion," as he called him. It was not long before the deserts and mountain regions of Lebanon, Mesopotamia, and Persia were filled with penitents and anchorites. Many of them still preferred to live as solitaries, but a growing number found comfort in the community life of the lauras. Under Hilarion's direction they began to build long cloister-like shelters with separate cells but a common refectory or dining room.

Now Hilarion had to begin traveling from one laura to another to advise, encourage, and, in considerable measure, control the monks as a superior or abbot. When he left one laura to go on to another, oftentimes the whole community went along with him part of the way so that they would not miss any of his teachings. It was not unusual for a thousand or more to follow him in this way. Naturally, a great many problems arose from this practice. Although each monk was responsible for his own provisions, it was inevitable that protests came from certain lauras that found themselves overrun by such armies of pilgrims.

One trouble was that, just as in Egypt, not all among those great multitudes of men were suited to the monastic life. Some of them were far from being good monks, or even good Christians. Hilarion used to send messengers on ahead to inform the brethren as to where he expected to spend the night. There was one monk who had a flourishing vineyard, and he had no mind to see hungry travelers eating his grapes. Some of the other brethren thought that he ought to be disciplined and suggested that Hilarion should stop there overnight. Hilarion said no because so many visitors would be a great burden to the brother and, furthermore, they would be lacking in charity themselves. Someone told the inhospitable brother, who felt ashamed and invited Hilarion and his disciples to spend the night with him. Hilarion accepted the invitation, but almost at once the monk regretted his impulsiveness. He gazed with affection upon his fine, large grapes. Then he set guards all about the vineyard with orders to drive away intruders with sticks, stones, or any weapons they could find.

The rest of the monks were very angry at such treatment, but Hilarion smiled tolerantly.

"It is not avarice that fills the barns and the wine casks," said Hilarion, "but the blessing of God. Let us go on to the dwelling of Brother Sabas."

Brother Sabas had a vineyard, too, and he had built his cell right in the middle of it. He worked very hard and produced good crops, but he gave nearly everything to the poor. Now he invited all the monks with Hilarion to come in and enjoy the grapes. They did so with great pleasure, and Hilarion blessed the vineyard with a special blessing. When the grapes were gathered that year, Brother Sabas had so many that he could hardly harvest them, but the miserly monk had no trouble at all. Most of his crop was shriveled and dry, and the grapes he did gather were sour.

Hilarion had not wanted to live among the people, but since that seemed to be God's will he made the best of it. He founded great numbers of cloisters and lauras, visiting them regularly and performing countless miracles. The nearby city of Gaza was almost completely pagan and many of the inhabitants hated and despised Hilarion because they feared him. One day, however, the Emperor Constantius sent to him from Byzantium, under protection of the Imperial Guard, a young soldier who was possessed of a devil. Much impressed by this sight, many curious citizens joined the procession, and when Hilarion cured the boy and refused the gold sent by the emperor, even the pagans knelt for his blessing.

All this contact with the world disturbed Hilarion. He was now sixty-three years old, and he feared that he would not have time to save his own soul. One day the woman whose sons he had saved long years before came to see him. She was on her way to visit Antony again, but Hilarion told her to wait.

"I, too, would have liked to join our father Antony once more, but it is too late for either of us now. We lost him yesterday. The news will soon arrive."

And the news did arrive. Hilarion grieved that he had not been able to visit Antony again. He wanted to go back to the desert himself, but the people flocked to him by thousands imploring him to stay. This time, however, Hilarion was firm. Too weak from fasting to walk, he asked for a donkey. He chose forty monks to go with him, blessed the weeping disciples, and started out on his journey. He visited all the monasteries and lauras once more and went by camel into the Egyptian desert to pray at Antony's cell.

Some time later the soldiers of the wicked Emperor Julian the Apostate appeared with orders to find the aged hermit and put him to death because he, like Antony, had preached against the Arian heresy. The soldiers burned down the cloisters and dispersed the monks. Hilarion was obliged to take ship for Sicily with only one companion. He had nothing with which to pay the captain but his book of Gospels which he always carried with him. The captain refused the old monk's book and allowed him to go on his journey, asking only for his blessing.

Hilarion found a cavern on the rocky coast, but as usual the people found him and brought the sick and afflicted for his healing. Meanwhile Hesychius, one of his most loyal disciples, had been searching for him everywhere. At last a Jewish merchant told him about a prophet who was preaching in Sicily and who would take no gifts or rewards for his miracles, saying only, "Freely have ye received; freely give."

Hesychius knew that the prophet must be Hilarion and found him easily because of the crowds who were following the old man on his donkey. Hilarion would not go back to Gaza, so Hesychius went with him to the island of Cyprus. There they remained for two years, living in the ruins of a pagan temple, but Hilarion was not satisfied. He would have liked to find some place in Egypt or Lybia where he could wait for death in peace, but he knew he would have no peace there. The faithful Hesychius finally found him a wild and solitary valley on the island. It was surrounded by great black rocks, but there was a pleasant meadow within, a clear stream, and even a little apple orchard.

Hilarion was now nearing eighty and, holy as his life had been, he feared the judgment of God. He comforted himself, however, as he had often comforted others and at length closed his eyes in peace with the faithful Hesychius at his side.

St. Antony taught the hermits and anchorites of the Egyptian desert how to live a community life in the lauras. St. Hilarion organized the monks of Palestine and Lybia and, going one step further, taught them to build cloisters and monasteries with many cells under one roof. So God's plan for the monastic life began to take shape and pattern through the teaching of the three great desert fathers, St. Paul, St. Antony, and St. Hilarion.

CHAPTER FOUR

St. Pachomius

The day was bitter cold and the company of young Roman soldiers were hungry and cruelly tired after the day's long march. Emperor Constantine had drafted all the best and strongest youths into his armies, and these boys who lived near the Nile in Egypt were huddled on the shore of that great river, waiting for a boat to take them to Alexandria. They were all less than twenty years of age, and they had been roughly treated by those in charge of them. As they sat there in dismal silence, one of them spoke suddenly.

"Torches!" he exclaimed. "Look! A company of men with torches. They are coming this way."

Nothing good had happened to the boys all day and they expected nothing now, but to their surprise the approaching men were laden with hot, comforting food for the young soldiers, and they talked to them so kindly and with such encouragement that the boys were very much touched. One young lad named Pachomius was especially grateful. He was a well-educated boy, the son of prosperous pagan parents, and he was little used to hardships.

"Who are these people?" asked Pachomius. "Why are they so kind to strangers?"

Pachomius learned that the men were Christians, that they followed the teachings of a prophet named Jesus Christ, Who said that He was the Son of God, and that they were kind and generous to all men but particularly to the sick or otherwise afflicted.

And now the hand of God reached down and touched the heart of the young soldier.

He went apart from the others for a moment and, folding his hands, he prayed earnestly that God would direct him.

"If Thou wilt deliver me from this present affliction and tell me how I may serve Thee," prayed Pachomius to the God he did not know, "I will do so all the rest of my life."

He had scarcely finished his prayer when the boat arrived and the soldiers were herded aboard to begin their time of duty in the emperor's service. It was a hard, rough life with many temptations, but Pachomius kept himself apart and never forgot his promise to God. In the year 313, the emperor's troops were victorious after a long war, and the soldiers were at last allowed to go home.

As soon as Pachomius reached his own dwelling place he became a catechumen, one of those who were studying the new religion that they might become Christians. He studied so diligently that very soon he was given the grace of baptism. Then Pachomius was so filled with love and happiness that he wanted to devote his whole life to the service of God, but he didn't know just how to go about it.

Now at that time there were already thousands of monks in the various deserts. Many of those trained by Antony and Hilarion had returned to their own neighborhoods and organized new lauras or cloisters and added individual ideas of their own. Most of the lauras had no fixed rules, but in Lower Egypt there was an anchorite named Ammon who had become the recognized leader in his neighborhood. The monks in his laura wove linen and sold it to get money for purposes of hospitality. They observed hours of prayer, work, and silence, and they ran a big central hospice for travelers and strangers, but the monks could come and go pretty much as they pleased and were not strictly bound.

Pachomius knew about Ammon's laura and approved of much that he saw there, but he was not attracted to that kind of life. He wanted to be a real solitary. Finally he heard about a very holy old anchorite named Palemon who lived far out in the desert. Pachomius determined to visit him, and after a long journey he found the hermit's hut. He knocked at the door, but he did not get a very warm reception.

"What do you want?" asked the old hermit severely.

Pachomius didn't think this was a very favorable beginning, but he tried again.

"The good God has sent me here," he said respectfully. "I want you to teach me how to serve God as an anchorite."

"How do I know that you are suited to the

life?" asked Palemon. "Many come. Many go. They tire of their prayers. They find it too difficult to fast. The life of an anchorite is not easy. It is very hard, indeed, and it should not surprise you that many grow weary of it. But it is very pleasing to God."

"Tell me about it, my father."

"It is lonely here. There is no one to help or serve the anchorite. I eat only bread and salt and a few herbs. Often I watch all night and meditate on the Holy Scriptures and on the goodness of God. In the daytime I work steadily. Idleness is a very grave sin."

Pachomius hesitated for a brief moment. He had so lately been a soldier and had endured so many hardships that he was sorely tempted to give up the idea of being an anchorite. Palemon made the life seem very difficult indeed. But God strengthened the boy's purpose. Pachomius straightened his back and held his head high.

"Christ the Lord will give me strength and patience to persevere," said Pachomius.

At first he had a very troublesome time. He was accustomed to sleeping well at night, and often now he fell asleep during the night watches, partly from habit and partly from sheer weariness. Palemon showed him how to keep himself awake by carrying a big sack of sand to and fro. Even that didn't always help. He was much worried by distractions, too.

"Aha!" nodded the old hermit understandingly. He knew all about it. "That is the way the Evil One seeks for admission to your soul. Don't give in or all our labor will go for nothing."

Pachomius didn't give in. He was so obedient and watchful that Palemon thanked God every day for sending him such a faithful disciple. And Pachomius thanked God for sending him to so holy a teacher.

After several years under Palemon's supervision, Pachomius decided to find a place where he could live alone, and he started out on his quest with Palemon's blessing. As he traveled along the course of the Nile River, he came to an ancient and beautiful temple which had been built by Cleopatra. The roof was supported by enormous columns, six in a row. It was being used at this time as a shelter for travelers. The floors were covered with layers of dried grass which served as bedding for man and beast. Outside were long clay watering-troughs and stone fireplaces in which travelers could build small fires to do their cooking. Many monks stopped there to rest on their way to visit some other anchorite or to find more suitable places for themselves. Pachomius did not stop, however. He feared the temptations of companionship.

As the young monk trudged along, staff in hand, he thought about the travelers' shelter that he had just seen and about the traveling monks' problem of finding shelter which would not subject them to the temptations of the world. He had not gone far when he came to a ruined village named Tabenna. It had once been a Christian settlement, but for some reason it had been abandoned. As Pachomius stood looking at it and wondering why the inhabitants had left their homes, he heard a voice: "Pachomius, this is the place where I wish you to serve Me." At the same moment an angel of the Lord stood by him and handed him a golden tablet on which were written a set of rules to be followed by monks living together in community.

Pachomius was not only surprised, but puzzled and a little frightened, at his encounter with the angel, but his only will was to do the will of God as exactly as possible. He hurried back to Palemon to ask for his advice. Palemon wasn't surprised. He had expected great things of his young pupil. He went back to Tabenna with Pachomius and gave him the best advice he could. Then he returned to his own little hut, very joyful and contented because God seemed to be well pleased with his beloved disciple. Only a short time afterward the old man died, and his last blessing was for the great work which he believed that Pachomius was about to commence.

Now Pachomius was alone; he had no one to depend upon but himself. He had not seen any member of his family since he had become a Christian, and he often wondered how they were faring. Then one day, soon after he had settled in Tabenna, his brother John suddenly appeared. Pachomius was astonished to learn that John had heard of him and of Palemon and that he had felt a great pride in his younger brother, so much so that he had decided to find Pachomius and share his desert life.

The two brothers were very happy together and led a rigidly penitential life. John was not even a Christian yet, but Pachomius instructed him thoroughly and he became an excellent monk. John was not as strong or as well-conditioned as his brother, however, and he did not live very long. Then Pachomius was alone again, but now he began to formulate a plan centered about the rules of life that the angel had given him. It became clear to him that he must gather all the anchorites who lived in the neighboring desert and teach them to live in community and to do productive work while at the same time carrying on their spiritual life.

It was the year 325 and Pachomius was about thirty-three years old when he founded the monastery of Tabenna. Both Antony of Egypt and Hilarion had been strong leaders and had ruled the communities they formed much as an abbot now does, but it was Pachomius who first used the word with the definite meaning of a superior or ruler of a community. The word abbot comes from the Greek word *abbas*, or father, and it is still in use today. Pachomius founded eight other monasteries besides the main one at Tabenna and put them all under one central government.

Not long after Pachomius had the monastery at Tabenna organized and functioning, one of his sisters came to visit him. She, too, was a convert. This was no happy meeting this time, however, as had happened when John arrived. Pachomius made it a rule never to speak to any woman, and he would make no exception for his sister even though it was a great sacrifice for both of them. But he did communicate with her through another monk and told her to assemble all the widows and young women who wished to lead holy lives in community and he would build a monastery for them across the river and draw up a rule for them.

In the year 328 a little group of women gathered in the new monastery on the bank of the Nile, and Pachomius sent a venerable monk known as Peter of Tabenna to instruct them and teach them how to observe the rules of poverty, chastity, obedience, and punctuality. They were allowed to see their fathers, brothers, or sons only very occasionally and always in the presence of their superior. They could not receive even the most trifling present from anyone. Any work that they could not do themselves was done by venerable and silent monks who always returned to Tabenna for meals. They were not allowed to accept even a drink of water from the nuns.

These first nuns were organized into a very well regulated community under the direction of Pachomius. There had been other loosely knit groups of holy women before this time, but they had had no formal rule. The nuns of the Tabenna monastery prayed several times a day in community and spent certain hours in the singing of psalms and in contemplation. They performed all the household duties such as cooking, baking, washing, working in the fields, spinning, and making garments for the poor.

In the beginning Pachomius was the sole servant of all the brothers. He was porter, gardener, cook, and infirmarian. Soon, however, there were hundreds of monks at Tabenna, and Pachomius spent most of his time in instruction. His monks had to spend three years in manual labor before they were allowed to begin their spiritual training. They could bring no money with them, nor could they receive presents. Anyone who could not read had to learn to do so, and they had to learn all of the psalms and the entire New Testament by heart. There were never enough books, so some of the monks spent all their time copying the Scriptures by hand. A trumpet called the monks to prayers, and they had to start immediately, no matter what they were doing. Pachomius believed strongly in punctuality.

Very few monks ever became priests. Antony, Hilarion, Ammon, Palemon, and Pachomius were all laymen. To this day, there are usually only a few monks in any community who are priests. Only as many are ordained as are necessary to serve the community. In the early monasteries the priests from the nearest village served the monks. If a priest wished to become a monk he had to be just like the others. All had to be brothers with no jealousy or envy. Obedience was another virtue cherished by Pachomius. The young novices were expected to obey instantly and willingly, no matter how little sense there seemed to be in the command given. Learning to subdue one's will was an important lesson to be learned.

All kinds of men came to Tabenna, and

they brought with them a great variety of gifts and skills. Some progressed very rapidly. Others seemed never to progress at all. Pachomius divided the monks into "orders." Each order had a leader. The whole monastery was divided into small units, each of which was under a prior. Gifted monks became the leaders while those with little skill were assigned to easier tasks. There were orders of cooks, gardeners, bakers, and porters. Each order had its own house, divided into cells. Three brothers lived in each cell. There was only one kitchen and one refectory. The monks ate in silence with the cowls of their habits pulled up over their heads so that no one could watch to see how much the others ate. The fare was neither rich nor abundant, but it was a long way from the bread and salt of St. Paul and St. Antony or the dried figs of Hilarion. There was bread and cheese with salt, fish, olives, figs, and fruits. The sick, the very old, and the young were allowed boiled vegetables, but those who were well were urged to practice self-denial. When they showed any lack of self-discipline, Pachomius actually wept in shame for them.

One of the important activities at Tabenna was a school for boys. The children were well taught and well fed. Once, when Pachomius had been away for two months, one of the boys said to him upon his return, "Only think, my father, while you have been gone, we have had no soup or vegetables to eat at all." Pachomius was much disturbed. He went to the kitchen and found the prior there plaiting mats.

"How long is it," asked Pachomius, "since you have had boiled vegetables or soup?"

"About two months," said the prior.

"Why?"

"Well, the monks rarely eat them, and it seemed better to save time and expense by plaiting mats to sell."

"How many mats have you made?"

"About five hundred."

"Bring them here."

When the mats had been brought, Pachomius called the community together and burned the mats before them.

"The prior has committed a grievous sin of disobedience," said he. "The rule prescribes certain kinds of food for the children and for the old or sick. They have been deprived of that food, and the brothers were deprived of a chance for self-denial. Let us keep the rule, my brothers."

Tabenna was the first monastery to be organized on such a large scale. Under the wise rule of Pachomius it became entirely self-supporting. A chief steward was in charge of business affairs. He kept two boats moving constantly up and down the Nile carrying supplies and goods to be marketed. The monks made quantities of the fine or coarse reed mats so necessary on the cold floors of Eastern houses. They were used also as sleeping pads, for shelter from the sun, and as awnings placed over stalls of merchandise in the marketplaces.

Each order had a library and a scriptorium where monks copied manuscripts on parchment, and a guest house was maintained near the monastery gate, where travelers and other guests were treated with great hospitality. Even to this day monasteries offer such hospitality to pilgrims and strangers. Tabenna was the first Christian order of monks, and the rule formulated by Pachomius was kept for centuries.

In the year 348 one of the great plagues that so often swept over the East struck Tabenna. More than a hundred monks died and among them was the holy abbot, Pachomius. Great was the grief of all the neighboring Christians, for Pachomius was dearly loved for his charity and humility. The lonely young soldier who had first learned of the teachings of Christ through the charity of Christian people had founded a community which was to be the forerunner of all religious orders, and he himself left an example for all time to those who enter religious life.

CHAPTER FIVE

St. Athanasius

The patriarch Alexander of Alexandria stood on the white-pillared porch of his house looking out across the sea. Down on the shore some small boys were playing, their short white tunics dancing against the blue of the water. Something about their movements caught the patriarch's attention. Several of the boys suddenly knelt on the sand, and a slightly-built redheaded boy made the sign of the cross over them. The patriarch was interested. He didn't think there were that many Christian children in this pagan neighborhood. Down to the beach he went to investigate.

The patriarch was even more astonished when he learned that the redheaded boy had just finished baptizing the others. He questioned the children and found them well instructed. He questioned the redhaired boy and decided that the baptisms were perfectly valid. What was the boy's name? Athanasius. The patriarch meditated. A boy of so much intelligence and zeal should be properly educated. Patriarch Alexander lost no time. He took the precocious young Athanasius into his own home and educated him for the priesthood.

Athanasius grew up small in stature. There was nothing impressive about his appearance, but he was a giant in intellect and character. Gentle and strong, but determined and uncompromising, his tongue and his pen were inspired, and he became one of the greatest glories of the Eastern Church.

In the early centuries, one of the persistent enemies of the Church was heresy. The Apostles handed on the teachings of Christ, complete and unchanged, to their successors, but as years went on human pride and vanity led certain leaders to deny particular truths and to preach false doctrines which contradicted the word of God and led to terrible controversies. One of the most violent of the early heresies was that known as Arianism which plagued the Church, especially in the East, for fifty years. Everyone took sides, and the quarrels were deep and bitter.

The Arian heresy was not a new one. It had arisen in the Church before, had been condemned by the bishops, and those who supported it had been expelled by the Church. Now, in the fourth century, a crafty and ambitious priest named Arius, who had hoped to be named patriarch of Alexandria, became angry and jealous when Alexander was elected. He wanted power and attention. Now he stood before his people and declared that Christ was not God. He told them that God the Son, the Second Person of the Blessed Trinity, could not be God in the same sense that the Father is God because He was created by the Father.

The people were shocked. This was a terrible thing to say. If Christ were not God, then He was only a creature like everyone else. How then could He redeem the world or found a church or teach true doctrine? After the first shock, some weak souls began to waver. Priests and bishops took sides. The Church was in turmoil. Most of the bishops of Egypt were against Arius. Patriarch Alexander deposed him and forbade him to preach.

Cast out of Egypt, Arius went to Syria where he found an ally. Bishop Eusebius, clever and crafty himself and no friend of Alexander, joined Arius. Unfortunately, Eusebius had gained considerable influence with Emperor Constantine, who interceded with Alexander to lift the ban on Arius. Alexander firmly refused, for now he had someone who stood like a rock beside him, and that was Athanasius. He was by this time secretary to Alexander and had traveled with the bishop all over the vast diocese, keeping his eyes and ears open. For a while he had stayed with some of the desert fathers and visited the famous Antony of Egypt. (It was then that he gave Antony the cloak that became so famous). He had seen much and studied much, and he had become a remarkably learned theologian well equipped to match wits with Arius. Eusebius and Arius were bitterly angry at Athanasius. They knew who supported the patriarch and saw through all their deceptions.

Emperor Constantine was disturbed. All these theological arguments were damaging to civil life. He thought of himself as a Christian although he had not yet been baptized. He wanted peace in his empire. The Western bishop, Hosius, who usually advised him on ecclesiastical matters, suggested that he call a universal council to discuss and settle some of these controversies once and for all. Constantine decided to do so. He appealed to Pope Sylvester to join him in summoning a council, and the Pope agreed willingly. The meeting place decided upon was Nicaea in Bithynia, Asia Minor, about twenty miles from Nicomedia. The year was 325.

That gathering of bishops turned out to be one of the great events in the history of the Church. It was the first ecumenical council ever called. Three hundred and eighteen bishops came from far and near, bringing priests, deacons, and acolytes. Official Western representatives were Theophilus the Goth and Hosius the Spaniard. They were given a place of honor and permitted to sign all documents before the others did. Representing the East were Macarius, bishop of Jerusalem, and Alexander of Alexandria with his young deacon Athanasius beside him. Only seventeen of the bishops present were on the side of Arius. Eusebius, of course, was one of them, and he was powerful because he was a friend of Emperor Constantine and his sister Constantia.

The great hall in which the council took place was a dramatic and colorful setting. In the center was a splendid throne upon which lay a copy of the Four Gospels as a symbol of the presence of Christ. There was a small gilt throne for the emperor, and rows of benches stood around the huge rectangle for the bishops and their retinues. After the bishops were assembled, Emperor Constantine made his entrance. He came almost dramatically alone, with only two attendants, but he wore on his shoulders the robe of imperial purple, heavy with gold and precious stones, and on his head the jeweled imperial crown. Constantine was aware that in spite of his rank he was only a catechumen in the midst of all these dignitaries, and he actually hesitated to ascend his throne until urged by the bishops. When he had done so, he addressed the gathering with royal dignity and pleaded for mutual peace and understanding. Then he sat down and the throng waited, tense with expectation.

The first to speak was Arius. A tall man of about sixty, he was thin and pale, with a wild shock of tangled hair. He was a frenzied and excitable preacher and capable of great persuasion. He had succeeded in building a reputation for great learning, eloquence, and sanctity, but on this occasion he revealed himself for what he was. Watching him intently was Athanasius the deacon, with his broad brow and keen eyes. It was said of him later that he looked like St. Michael ready to strike.

"Jesus Christ is not God," shouted Arius. The bishops cried out in horror and indignation. The wily Eusebius saw that Arius had made a mistake. He rose to cover it up.

"What Arius means," he said in a conciliatory tone, "is that Jesus Christ is *nearly*, but not *quite* God."

The other bishops were not appeased. They murmured angrily. Arius continued his argument. Then Alexander made a small sign and Athanasius leaped to his feet. He answered Arius in such inspired words that everyone who heard him marveled. Arius was disclaimed in vehement terms, and a committee was appointed to draw up a profession of faith.

The writing of such a document was a delicate matter. Certain words had to be defined clearly and the beliefs of the Church stated in terms that could not be misunderstood. At last Bishop Hosius put into final form a profession of faith that seemed to embody all the controversial issues. One very important word is said to have been contributed by Athanasius. That word is *consubstantial*, which carries the meaning that the Son is of one substance, one nature, one essence with the Father and equal to Him. That creed, formulated at the first ecumenical council, held in Nicaea, became what is known as the Nicene Creed. To this day it is the profession of faith of the entire Catholic world and is found in every prayer book and missal as the *Credo* of the Mass.

The new creed was signed by every bishop present except the seventeen Arians who had come to support their leader. The emperor promised to uphold the laws of the Church by means of the laws of the state. That made some of the Arians waver. Finally all signed but five. The emperor hinted at banishment and sent a message to Eusebius urging him to give in. At length, Eusebius and his friend Theognis of Nicaea apparently yielded. They signed last of all but not before Eusebius, with a quick stroke of his pen, had changed the Greek word for *substance* to one meaning *like in substance*.

Emperor Constantine, then in the twentieth year of his reign, was well pleased with the results of his efforts and entertained the bishops at a great banquet. Meanwhile Eusebius and Theognis bribed some guards to let them see the document they had just signed and erased their names from the Profession of Faith. When the deception was discovered three months later, they were both banished by Constantine, who was hurt and angry to find himself thus deceived.

At length the good patriarch Alexander died and Athanasius, who by now had been ordained a priest, fled in consternation fearing that he might be named to succeed Alexander. His flight was in vain for the people elected him by proclamation, praying with uplifted hands: "Give us Athanasius! God, give us Athanasius!" The council of bishops agreed. Athanasius was only thirty years old, but he had the wisdom and experience of a much older man. In spite of his reluctance he was obliged to accept the charge.

The first few years of his rule were comparatively peaceful for Athanasius. He would have been very happy if he could have retired to the desert to live as a solitary, but he knew that such a life was not God's will for him. By this time Pachomius had his monastery at Tabenna well established and, having heard much of Athanasius, he came down one day with some of his monks to visit the bishop and ask for his blessing. Pachomius, always modest and humble, hid among his monks, but Athanasius was not deceived. He recognized Pachomius at once and they became firm friends. In the years of trial ahead, Athanasius was more than once to be grateful for the friendship of the desert monks who were always faithful in his service.

Peace did not last long. Constantia, the

emperor's sister, who was still a friend of Arius, persuaded her brother to recall Eusebius and Theognis from exile and they soon began to exert their old influence over him. They deposed the bishops who had replaced them, gathered new followers, and began persecuting Athanasius, now patriarch of Alexandria, with such venom that even the aged St. Antony heard about it in his distant desert cell and came down to Alexandria to encourage Athanasius. He blessed the crowds who came to hear him and exhorted them to have nothing to do with the Arians.

Eusebius kept up his persecution, hurling unjust and malevolent charges at Athanasius and lying to the emperor until Constantine was persuaded to banish the bishop to Gaul. He refused, however, to name any successor, and Athanasius ruled as patriarch from his place of exile.

Meanwhile the people were protesting vehemently. Finally, they fasted and prayed for seven days. On the last day Arius arrived in Alexandria. His supporters formed a procession of great grandeur and escorted the heretic around the city in triumph. The people continued to weep and pray in the streets. Suddenly the procession halted. Arius had become violently ill. He was hurried away quickly by his friends and the procession disbanded, but the news of his horrible death soon seeped out and the awe-struck people saw in it the judgment of God.

Emperor Constantine was much impressed by this remarkable event. He did not live much longer himself, but on his deathbed he sent word to his eldest son Constantine to restore Athanasius to his see, and he sent for Eusebius to baptize him. It was a common and dangerous custom in those days for rulers and persons of high rank to defer baptism until they were well beyond middle age or even until they were actually in danger of death. But it does seem ironic that the well-intentioned Constantine should have received the sacrament from so unworthy a hand as that of Eusebius. He was still a bishop, however, no matter how unworthy, and the baptism was valid.

After Constantine's death the empire was divided among his three sons, Constantine II, Constans, and Constantius. The first two died within two years, and the third, Constantius, was a weak man, a tool of the Arians, and an enemy of Athanasius. Constantine II had recalled the patriarch to Alexandria as his father had directed, but under Constantius new troubles began.

There was no end to the persecutions. Many innocent bishops were scourged, tortured, and sent into exile. One winter's day Bishop Athanasius was sitting on his episcopal throne in the church of St. Theonas. Suddenly there were shouts and cries and the doors were battered down by an army of five thousand men who surrounded the church with orders to take the patriarch dead or alive. Athanasius remained calm. He ordered the deacons to proceed with the psalm and afterwards to leave the church quietly.

"O praise the Lord for He is good," began the deacons.

"For His mercy endureth forever," answered the people.

"Praise ye the God of Gods."

"For His mercy endureth forever."

Meanwhile the people nearest Athanasius urged him to escape.

"No," said the patriarch. "The shepherd's place is with his flock."

Now the soldiers rushed upon him with drawn swords. Some of the frightened people fled. Many were trampled underfoot or slain by the soldiers. Athanasius refused to move, but in the confusion some of the monks and the clergy picked him up and carried him out straight through the crowds of soldiers who were searching for him.

Angered by the escape of Athanasius, Emperor Constantius imprisoned or exiled nearly all the bishops who had signed the Nicene

Creed. Once more, St. Antony, now on his deathbed, sent words of hope and encouragement to Athanasius. He sent also one of his own sheepskin garments in return for the one Athanasius had given him so long before, and with it his last blessing.

Again the people of Alexandria clamored for their bishop. The emperor punished them for their loyalty by desecrating their churches, burning sacred books, and torturing priests and holy women. But Constantius died and was succeeded by the notorious Julian the Apostate. Julian, who had been brought up as a Christian, now threw off any pretense to religion. He declared himself a pagan, rebuilt the temples of the gods, and offered sacrifice to them; and he bribed Christians to become apostates like himself.

When Athanasius did return to Alexandria, hoping to persuade the weaker Arians to return to the Church, he found the city full of magicians, diviners, and fortunetellers who had come at Julian's invitation. Now they complained that Athanasius was ruining their trade. Julian again condemned Athanasius to exile. Again the people protested. Julian replied by ordering Athanasius put to death. Warned by his people, Athanasius fled by boat, but he went only a little way up the river and then turned back.

One of the imperial boats came by at great speed, propelled by sweating oarsmen.

"How far off is Athanasius?" shouted an officer.

"Quite close," Athanasius shouted back. "Keep going."

They did. So did Athanasius. He remained hidden in the city for a few days and then went to the monastery at Tabenna to seek shelter with Pachomius. He was still there when word came of the death of Emperor Julian in battle. Now Athanasius could return to his beloved city, for the next emperor, Jovian, was a Christian; but he, unfortunately, lived only a short time and was succeeded by two brothers, Valentinian in the West and Valens in the East. Valens was a weak and cruel man who had an Arian wife. Almost at once, persecutions began again.

On one evil day eighty priests and clerics who had been condemned to exile were placed on a ship, and the ship was set afire. Again Athanasius escaped. He hid for four months in his father's tomb, but at length he was permitted to return to his see. He was frail now and in constant ill health as a consequence of his many hardships, but his inspired pen was never idle.

When Damasus I became Pope, succeeding Liberius, he called a great synod of Church leaders, and a decree was issued that henceforth no bishop could be consecrated anywhere in the Christian Church unless he held to the creed of Nicaea. That was a great triumph for Athanasius in his old age and a strong blow against Arianism.

Athanasius governed the Church in Alexandria for nearly fifty years. He was eighty years old when God finally called him to enjoy the peace he had never known on earth. He was a truly great man, modest and unassuming in spite of his remarkable gifts. Athanasius was the first and probably the greatest of the Greek Fathers, those mighty defenders of the Church against heresy, and he is highly honored in the Western Church as well as in the East. In the Latin liturgy his feast occurs on May 2. The words of the Introit of the Mass for that day are a tribute to his greatness:

In the midst of the Church the Lord opened his mouth and filled him with the spirit of wisdom and understanding. He clothed him with a robe of glory.

CHAPTER SIX

St. Basil the Great

"Basil's the last! Basil's the last!"

Basil was always the last. Plagued by ill health all his life, he was no good at wrestling, or running races, or throwing javelins. The younger boys were all stronger and hardier, and even the girls could beat him. There were ten children in Basil's family, five boys and five girls, and of the ten four became saints, not to mention the father, mother, and two grandmothers. They were quite a remarkable family.

It was in the year 329 in the town of Caesarea in Cappadocia that Basil was born. Cappadocia was in Asia Minor. Basil was the second child and first son of a wealthy and highly regarded young Christian couple who were well established in a large, comfortable mansion with dozens of household servants to wait upon them. Basil, the father, was a man who prized scholarship, and the mother, Emmelia, was a gracious and beautiful woman of excellent education. As the children came along, they were well taught and well disciplined. Although they had many tutors, the parents supervised closely every aspect of their education.

Another strong influence in the lives of Basil's family was their grandmother (their father's mother), known as Macrina the elder because her eldest grandchild was named for her. She lived in a big country house which the children loved to visit. There the younger boys hunted, fished, and rode horseback while Basil found a quiet corner to read and study.

Macrina the elder was an excellent storyteller, and so was Emmelia. Between them they saw to it that the children were well trained in religion and literature and that they had the Scriptures and the Greek classics at the tip of their tongues. The father instructed them in logic. He wanted his sons, especially, to think clearly and to be able to express themselves eloquently and forcefully in argument and debate.

"Of what use is it to read and write," he was often heard to say, "if you can't think and reason?"

By the time Basil was sixteen he was a well-trained scholar with a precocious mind and it was time for him to begin his higher studies. The sons of distinguished families were usually sent to Constantinople or Athens. There were good schools in Caesarea, but there was a tendency to regard them as rather countrified. They lacked the glamour of the greater cities. The schools of Constantinople were, however, relatively new and untried. Athens was the real center of learning.

The trouble with Athens was that it was a city dangerous to Christian faith because of its Greek paganism. It was very important to gifted young men to have the advantage of Greek scholarship. The courses in history, philosophy, and art were matchless, but the Christian student paid a heavy price for them. The Greeks disliked Christians. They called them barbarians and enemies of Hellenism and said tauntingly that they worshipped a Jew. Nevertheless many Christian students suffered the hardships and dangers for the sake of the excellent training and the prestige gained by those who studied in Athens.

Before Basil went to Athens, he and his brother Gregory studied for some time in the schools of Caesarea. There Basil met another Gregory, who was also to become a saint. Gregory Nazianzen, so called because he came from the small town of Nazianzus in Cappadocia, was also a brilliant student. He and Basil became fast friends almost at once and soon were quite inseparable. Later Basil went on to Constantinople for further study while Gregory Nazianzen went to Palestine and Alexandria, but they eventually met again in Athens.

There was glory, beauty, and opportunity in the storied city of Athens with its temples, its statues, its olive groves, and its wine-dark sea celebrated by Homer. The two boys were well aware of the dangers they faced, and they attended strictly to business. It was said of them later that they knew only two streets, the one to church and the one to school. They studied history, philosophy and logic, mathematics, astronomy, and medicine, but their favorite subject was rhetoric. It gave them a sense of power to be able to use words so eloquently that they could teach, persuade, or convince at will. Gregory Nazianzen said of his friend

Basil that he was "equipped with all the learning attainable by the nature of man" and Basil was, indeed, one of the most distinguished scholars in the Athens of his time.

A good many of the young students in Athens led anything but exemplary lives, but Basil and Gregory avoided the pagans and gloried in the name of Christian, although they were persecuted because of it. Among their classmates was a young man to whom they both took a strong dislike for his arrogance, affectation, and extravagance. They had little to do with him then, but they had good reason to know him later as the Roman emperor, Julian the Apostate, a bitter foe of Christianity.

By the time Basil returned to Caesarea, his father and his grandmother were dead and four of his sisters married. The eldest sister, Macrina, had been betrothed at an early age but when the young man died she refused all other suitors and remained at home to help her mother with the younger children. Peter, the youngest (later to be known as St. Peter of Sebaste), was always her special charge. The third boy, who eventually became St. Gregory of Nyssa, had also married and was at this time a teacher of rhetoric.

Macrina was of an intensely religious nature. She was disturbed at Basil's apparent conceit and self-importance and feared that Athens had left its mark. Her brother Gregory, although he was a good solid Christian, worried her, too. He had become quite an orator and seemed a little too worldly. He grew restless during overlong family prayers and was inclined to resent Macrina's solicitude. Basil had a fine steady character, but he enjoyed his distinguished reputation, and it seemed to Macrina that all he lived for was glory and admiration. He became the head of all the schools and colleges in Caesarea and taught a highly popular course in rhetoric, but Macrina kept after him. She was only a year older than he, but she still had a strong influence over him. She thought that he ought to be something greater than a teacher of rhetoric. Besides, he wasn't even baptized.

Macrina must have had a pretty good command of rhetoric herself. At any rate she persuaded Basil that he was destined for something more important in the sight of God than worldly popularity and honors. In the year 357 he was baptized, and he decided at once that he would become a monk.

There were thousands of monks now living in the deserts. The great St. Antony of Egypt had died only the year before. Hilarion, Palemon, Ammon, and others had made a beginning of organized community life, and Pachomius had established his very successful monastery at Tabenna. Basil determined to study the monastic way of life and to learn all he could from those famous teachers. He had some ideas himself. He thought that there ought to be stronger discipline to hold the monks together.

For two years Basil traveled all over Egypt, Palestine, and Syria and studied with the holiest teachers he could find. Then he returned to Cappadocia to begin his own life as a monk. He chose a beautiful spot on the shore of the river Iris in the near-by province of Pontus near the Black Sea. With its flowers, birds, and wooded hills it was a veritable haven of peace. Since his mother and his sister Macrina no longer had any family responsibilities, they assembled their friends and servants, and Basil helped them establish a colony for women on the opposite bank of the Iris. His youngest brother, Peter, now grown up, became his own first disciple. Basil's monastery was the first in Asia Minor.

Basil wrote at once to Gregory Nazianzen and asked him to come and help organize the new community.

"That town you live in is full of bears and wolves and mud," he wrote jokingly. "You who so love beauty will be happy in this peaceful spot."

Gregory Nazianzen was only too happy to come although his father, who was bishop of

Nazianzus, objected strongly. Soon a large colony of monks gathered around them. The life was hard. The monks did everything for themselves. They dug, planted, plowed, harvested, and built their shelters with their own hands. Each monk had one tunic and one cloak, and they slept on the bare ground. They had a common roof and a common table, and they prayed, chanted, and worked in common, although strict silence was required otherwise, except for necessity. Basil made many new rules. He did not believe in excessive fasting, for example. The monks took no vows, but each one was placed under strict obligation to keep the rules with regard to prayer, work, and personal sanctification.

Basil believed strongly that it was not sufficient for monks just to live holy lives. They must do good actively. He therefore founded orphanages and schools and taught the monks how to be good teachers. He believed in creating interest in a subject and making education a challenge, and he advocated firm but gentle discipline rather than force. When he found exceptionally talented children he sent them outside for special training. For five years he ruled his monastery wisely and well, and then he was obliged to go back into the world to do his part in fighting the scourge of Arianism.

The emperor at this time was Julian the

Apostate whom Basil remembered well. Julian supported the Arians and he hated Caesarea, and all Cappadocia for that matter, because it was so completely Christian. He persecuted the citizens by means of taxes, confiscation of property, and cruel punishments. Some of the weaker bishops gave in and signed the Arian creed to save themselves. The bishop of Caesarea was a weak, fearful, and uncertain man. Basil became his right hand, strengthening, encouraging, and defending him. The bishop ordained Basil a priest, and after that Basil was a sort of vicar-general to the bishop and a veritable tower of resistance against heresy, as the next emperor, Valens, was soon to learn.

Always a teacher and a reformer, Basil now turned his attention to other matters that he thought could be improved. He shortened the liturgy and reformed the church services so effectively that to this day the Liturgy of St. Basil is used in Eastern Rite churches on many Sundays and feast days during the year, while the one used for most other occasions is that of St. John Chrysostom, a shortened form of St. Basil's Liturgy. His liturgical reforms in the East rank with those of St. Gregory the Great in the West.

In spite of his strong character, Basil was a deeply humble man. He used great tact with the bishop, who was very jealous of his assistant although he could not do without him. Basil gave the bishop credit for everything and spent himself in the service of the poor. He had a decided instinct for social service, and when the district was stricken by a terrible famine, following a crop failure, Basil set up public kitchens, open alike to pagan, Jew, or Christian, and he himself put on an apron and fed the starving people.

Eventually Basil became metropolitan of Caesarea. (Metropolitans, patriarchs and exarchs were all bishops whose titles varied according to the size, location and importance of their sees.) Basil ruled over a vast territory comprising Cappadocia, Pontus, Galatia, and Armenia—in fact, nearly all of northern and central Asia Minor. He ruled this great territory for nine years and was one of the most powerful of the younger men who took up the work of the mighty Athanasius against heresy.

When Valens became emperor and tried to make the whole empire Arian, Basil stood firm against him. So eloquently did he preach that Valens, filled with curiosity, as well as fury, went to Caesarea to see this man who defied him. On the feast of the Epiphany he entered Basil's church and found him sitting on his episcopal throne. Basil was a tall, pale, thin man with a long beard. He did not look very formidable, but Valens was nevertheless impressed. When it was time for the Offertory, the emperor approached the throne with his gift, just as the other people did, and to everyone's surprise Basil accepted it graciously.

Not long after this incident, the emperor's son Galatos lay dying, and his mother implored Valens to send for Basil. Valens did so most reluctantly, and Basil went immediately to the palace. He cured the boy at once, but he warned Valens that God would allow this miracle only if the boy were baptized a Catholic. Valens promised, but he kept only half of the promise. He had the boy baptized an Arian. Galatos died immediately afterward. Valens angrily determined to banish Basil, but every time he raised his hand to sign the document his reed pen broke and his hand became paralyzed. Valens changed his mind, and Basil remained in Caesarea.

On another occasion Valens had handed a Catholic church over to the Arians. Basil protested vehemently. At last Valens closed and sealed the church. Then he said that it would belong to the side that succeeded in opening the doors by prayer. The Arians tried first. They prayed for three days, but the doors remained closed. Basil then led his clergy to the entrance and prayed. He touched the doors lightly with his pastoral crook, and they opened wide. Valens had to keep his word, and the church went back to the Catholics.

Basil was a true shepherd to his flock. He established institutions for his sick and needy, and for strangers and pilgrims. He provided training for unskilled workers and taught the rich to help the poor with generosity and prudence. When people complained that they could not give, he scolded them.

"You refuse to give because you haven't enough for your own requirements," he said in a sermon, "but while your tongue excuses, your hand condemns. The price of that ring on your finger declares you to be a liar. It would release many prisoners or clothe many ill-clad people, yet you turn away the poor empty-handed. Give your last loaf of bread to the beggar at your door and trust in God."

Gentle as he was, Basil could be severe with hypocrites and sinners, and he was very strict with his clergy. His diocese was a model of ecclesiastical discipline. His health was always poor and his duties heavy, but he became one of the chief classical writers of the fourth century and still found time to write fascinating letters to his friends. His long friendship with Gregory Nazianzen, however, was clouded toward the end. It was Basil's fault in a way. He could be very arbitrary when occasion demanded action. Having great need of reliable bishops, he consecrated his reluctant brother Gregory for the undesirable diocese of Nyssa, and he wanted Gregory Nazianzen for another trouble spot. Gregory Nazianzen had never even wanted to be a priest and he absolutely refused to become a bishop, but Basil insisted, and from then on Gregory drew away from his old friend and never quite forgave him.

In the year 379, when he was only forty-nine, worn out by work, ill health, and austerities, Basil lay on his deathbed. When he heard, however, that many candidates were awaiting ordination as deacons and priests, he rose with a great effort and ordained them. Then he went back to bed to die.

The whole city followed Basil to his grave. His body was borne on an open bier through the streets, and the people crowded close to touch his garments. Gregory of Nyssa preached the funeral sermon and paid a touching tribute to his brother. Gregory Nazianzen was grief-stricken, but he was too sick himself to attend the funeral. He wrote a beautiful letter to Gregory of Nyssa, however, and two years later preached an eloquent panegyric on the character and achievements of his old friend.

St. Basil was one of the great figures in Christian history. He ranks with St. Benedict in the annals of monasticism, establishing a rule that was outstanding in prudence and wisdom. He was an early champion of social justice, an ardent defender against heresy, a brilliant liturgist, and an educator far ahead of his time.

Every year in both East and West, St. Basil the Great is remembered. His own Byzantine Church keeps his feast on January the first, the day of his death. The Roman Church celebrates the day of his consecration, June the fourteenth. On that day she praises the name of

> *. . . St. Basil, Bishop, who at the time of the Emperor Valens, shone with wonderful wisdom and knowledge, was adorned with all virtues, and defended the Church with unchanging constancy against the Arians and Macedonians.*

CHAPTER SEVEN

St. Gregory Nazianzen

Gregory Nazianzen was a reserved and thoughtful man, sensitive, poetic, shy, and inclined to solitude. He would have liked nothing better than to retire to some desert place and remain there all his life, fasting, praying, and serving God as a monk or a hermit. Instead, he was constantly being pushed into the middle of arguments and controversies and forced into a public life which he hated. He spent a large part of his life in the midst of bitter conflict.

From the time they went to school together, Gregory looked up to his friend Basil as one who was capable of knowing and understanding everything that there was for man to know. Yet he himself is regarded as one of the great intellects of the early centuries. He is a Doctor of the Church, surnamed the Theologian; and he is honored as one of the greatest of the Greek Fathers. These titles may need a little explanation.

The term "Fathers of the Church" applies to those early Christian leaders of great sanctity and scholarship who taught and preached the true doctrine and preserved it in their writings. The age of the Fathers began right after the age of the Apostles and continued up to the beginning of the Middle Ages. The so-called Desert Fathers were outstanding hermits or monks who attracted many followers by reason of their teaching and example. Most of them were more famous for preaching than for writing. The Greek Fathers were eminent writers and preachers of the Byzantine Church who wrote and spoke in Greek, which was the common language of learning and of the liturgy.

The Fathers of the Church usually acquired that title by reason of the judgment of the contemporary Church and of the people, supported by the opinion of the saints and scholars who came after them. Doctors of the Church, however, can be named only by the Pope himself or by a general council of the Church. Only theologians of the highest rank and sanctity, thoroughly versed in sacred law, the Scriptures, and all aspects of religion, are so honored—such men as St. Ambrose, St. Augustine, and St. Jerome of the Roman Church and St. Athanasius, St. Basil the Great, and St. John Chrysostom of the Byzantine Church. Gregory Nazianzen belongs to that select group.

But even a Doctor of the Church has to be born somewhere, and Gregory Nazianzen was born in the little village of Arianzus in Cappadocia, which can be found on the old maps up north of Palestine along the Black Sea. His family must have moved shortly afterward to Nazianzus because Gregory always bore that name. Names like Gregory and Basil were so common that those who bore them often had to add the name of their home towns for identification. It would save a great deal of confusion if we knew their family names, but they used a different system in those days.

Gregory's parents were Gregory the Elder and Nonna, a very good Christian woman, who probably prayed her pagan husband into the Church and even beyond, for he soon became a priest and later a bishop. In the Eastern Church a man already married could be ordained, although he could not marry after his ordination. When a married man became a priest, quite frequently the couple would separate, and the wife would enter some community of holy women. It is probable that Gregory and Nonna did separate, at least after their two sons were well grown. We do know for certain that both of them became saints.

The two boys attended the schools in Caesarea in Cappadocia, then a center of learning, where the long friendship of Basil and Gregory began. The two younger boys in each family —Basil's brother, Gregory Nyssa, and young Caesarius of Nazianzus—were probably classmates, too. Caesarius studied medicine and became court physician in Constantinople under Constantius II. When he died, Gregory of Nyssa preached his funeral sermon. All four of the boys became saints.

Rhetoric and oratory were Gregory's favorite subjects. He had an inclination to the law as a profession, and the best law schools were supposed to be in Alexandria or in Palestine. He and Basil were loath to part, but they consoled each other with the promise that they would surely meet again in Athens. Basil, who was planning rather vaguely to be a rhetor, or teacher, was going to Constantinople for the next step in his training. Both boys considered themselves Christians and led strict Christian lives, but neither had yet been baptized.

The common practice at that time of deferring baptism until late in life probably sprang from the conviction that baptism would wash away all sins committed previous to that event, whereas those committed after baptism might not be forgiven so easily and would certainly incur heavy penance. If they waited until almost the last minute, many people reasoned, they need not be so strict with themselves and the long-deferred sacrament would take them right into heaven. It was a dangerous practice, eventually suppressed, but remembering the very severe penances imposed on the early Christians, it is easy to understand their point of view.

At all events, when at last Gregory had finished his course in law and started the long voyage to Athens he was still unbaptized and had good cause to regret it. The small vessel on which he had taken passage had a rough voyage all the way, and at one point encountered a tempest so violent that it seemed hardly possible for the ship to survive. It was then that Gregory began to wonder what would happen to his soul if he were summoned before God at that moment. He made a resolution to seek baptism as soon as he reached Athens, but like a good many other people, as soon as the sun shone again he forgot his fears and his resolutions and, as a matter of fact, was not baptized until he reached home again several years later.

When Gregory and Basil left Athens they were both about thirty. Basil, of course, came under the influence of his sister Macrina and was baptized not long after he reached home. It is believed that Gregory Nazianzen had some sort of deep religious experience and was probably baptized at about the same time. He decided to give up the idea of practicing law and returned to Nazianzus where his father, now a bishop, needed his help.

At this point Basil started his monastery on the river Iris and sent for his friend to join him. Gregory's father protested. He was getting old and the work of the diocese was too much for him. When he saw how eager his son was, however, he finally consented—but for a limited time only. Gregory spent two happy, fruitful years with Basil, planning and building the monastery and working out a rule. Then his father called him back.

Gregory did not want to leave the monastery at all. He was a born monk. The life just suited him. But when his father insisted upon ordaining him a priest he was shocked, angry, and desperate. He did not feel worthy to be a priest, and he just couldn't face the problems that he could easily foresee. He ran away from the whole unhappy situation and went back to Basil's community. For ten weeks he prayed and struggled with temptation, but from the first he knew that he would have to return. Later on he wrote a beautiful treatise on the priesthood by way of apology for his reluctance to enter that state.

In the year 370 Basil, who had also had to give up his happy life as a monk, had been made metropolitan of Caesarea. Now he was having trouble with Emperor Valens. He needed good, solid, dependable bishops in a number of key areas, and he had already made his own brother, Gregory, bishop of Nyssa in spite of his protests. He had been keeping his eye on Gregory Nazianzen for some time, too. Gregory's father had gone a little too far in conciliating the Arians and had thereby offended the monks of the neighborhood. Gregory Nazianzen, however, had been very successful in restoring peace to the troubled province. Basil therefore made him bishop of Sasima, a miserable, unhealthful, out-of-the-way place, but nevertheless important. He did it without his friend's consent, and Gregory was deeply hurt as well as angry. He absolutely refused to go near the place, and from that time on their friendship was never the same.

Gregory still wanted to be a monk, but he had to stay with his aged father, now nearly one hundred years old, and he acted as coadjutor in Nazianzus as long as his father lived. After the old bishop's death, Gregory's health broke down entirely. He retired to Seleucia in a near-by province that climbed the slopes of the Taurus Mountains. There for five years he succeeded in living the kind of quiet, secluded life that suited him, but this interval of peace was not to last.

The death of Emperor Valens was a great blessing to the Christians. The new emperor, Theodosius, was himself a Christian, and an era of peace began in the empire. The Church in Constantinople, however, was in a very bad condition. Arianism had made tremendous inroads there because it had for so long been supported by the emperors. There were actually only a few Catholics left in the city and they were disorganized. They sent for Gregory Nazianzen to come to the capital city and restore order.

Gregory was naturally very reluctant to go. He knew well that he would have to face confusion, argument, even violence, and he disliked intensely the corruption that he knew had become a part of life in the capital. When he finally did go, because he felt that he must, he was very badly received by the people. They were accustomed to great splendor in both Church and State, and here was a man, bald and poorly dressed, bent with illness, and looking little indeed like a bishop. They felt cheated and a little ashamed.

Since no bishop's palace was offered him, Gregory went to live with some relatives and chose the small church of St. Anastatia outside the city for his parish. There he began to preach. Gregory was a powerful speaker. Only a few came at first, but those few were astonished and impressed. His congregation increased, and his sermons on the Trinity drew great audiences. The Arians were dismayed as they saw the old faith being restored to the city. They did everything they could to interfere with his work. They insulted and ill-treated him and defiled his church, but Gregory's influence grew. It was not long before he won the esteem of the best scholars and thinkers in the city.

It happened about this time that St. Jerome, probably the most learned scholar of his age, was returning from the desert of Syria where he had been living for some time as a solitary. Having heard of Gregory's eloquence and learning, he stopped in Constantinople to learn all he could from so holy a man. Nor was he disappointed. It was a meeting of two great minds and two great saints, for Jerome, who was to become one of the most distinguished doctors of the Western Church, was even then a champion of religious liberty, and a fearless opponent of Arianism; and Gregory Nazianzen would be known in time as one of the "Three Torches of the East." Jerome greatly admired the Eastern Fathers, and his statue in St. Peter's in Rome shows him together with St. Augustine (whose conversion he completed after it was begun by St. Antony of Egypt), St. Athanasius, and St. John Chrysostom holding up St. Peter's chair. St. Gregory Nazianzen should have been with them for he was their equal.

In the year 380 Emperor Theodosius issued an edict that all Byzantine subjects should observe the Catholic faith as professed by the Pope of Rome and the Archbishop of Alexandria. Angry and baffled, the Arians left the city. The following year the emperor called the second ecumenical council for the purpose of strengthening the Christian faith, reaffirming the doctrines denied by the Arians, and fortifying the position of the Christians in Constantinople who, under Gregory's influence, had multiplied and become strong and faithful. Now, at the wish of the council over which he had presided and at the urgent persuasion of Emperor Theodosius, Gregory accepted the post of patriarch of Constantinople. He was solemnly consecrated in the beautiful cathedral of the Holy Wisdom, but again peace was denied him. In spite of the emperor's edict there was still a sufficient number of Arian sympathizers in the city to stir up trouble. The validity of Gregory's election was questioned, and other charges brought against him.

Gregory was tired of fighting. He had not wanted to go to Constantinople in the first place. He had not wanted to be a bishop. He had kept the faith burning in Constantinople in that city's darkest hours. Now he just wanted to find some quiet place in which to end his days. He preached a very touching farewell sermon and left the city gladly to return to Cappadocia.

For the rest of his life Gregory led the kind of life that he had always wanted. He wore a monk's habit and sandals, spent most of his time reading, writing, and studying, and had a small garden which gave him much satisfaction. In spite of the fact that his health was always precarious, he imposed on himself many acts of penance and mortification, such as never having a fire in his room no matter how cold it was. He left a great treasury of writings in prose and poetry which are very highly regarded, not only for their theological importance, but because Gregory was a true master of style. He was a man of great virtue and keen intellect, eloquent of speech and persuasive in writing, but he had the humble heart of a monk.

The Western Church honors St. Gregory Nazianzen on May ninth, and the Epistle read in the Mass of that day is particularly appropriate:

> . . . *For if it shall please the great Lord, he will fill him with the spirit of understanding; and he will pour forth the words of his wisdom as showers, and in his prayer he will confess to the Lord. And the Lord will direct his counsel, and his knowledge, and in his secrets shall he meditate. He will show forth the discipline he has learned, and will glory in the covenant of the Lord. Many will praise his wisdom, and it will never be forgotten. The memory of him will not depart away, and his name will be in request from generation to generation. Nations will declare his wisdom, and the Church will show forth his praise.*

CHAPTER EIGHT

St. Gregory of Nyssa

St. Gregory of Nyssa is one of the most interesting saints in the Byzantine calendar. The younger brother of St. Basil the Great, he always walked in his shadow. Since he bore the same name as St. Gregory Nazianzen, his brother's friend, and was overshadowed by him also, the real merits of Gregory Nyssa always tended to be overlooked.

Gregory was the third son of St. Basil the

Elder and St. Emmelia. The exact year of his birth is uncertain, but he came about halfway down in the family of ten. As a small child he was taught by his oldest sister, Macrina, who had a great deal of teaching skill. Macrina was a person of character even as a child. She resembled her remarkable grandmother, Macrina the elder, having the same powerful, penetrating mind and prodigious memory. She was only thirteen when her father died. When the youngest child, Peter, was born almost at the same time, she took charge of him and became companion and helper to her mother. She seems to have taken over the whole household, waiting on her invalid mother, teaching and caring for the other children, and managing the large estate.

Basil and Gregory attended school for some time in Caesarea, but when Basil went on to Constantinople, and later to Athens, Gregory apparently was satisfied with the education available in Caesarea. He was very fond of Basil and admired his brilliance, but he himself did not have the spirit of competition. He loved rhetoric and oratory as did all the children in that remarkable family; still he was content to be just a lector in the church although he did become a reader, probably urged on by Macrina, and he took a post as a secular teacher of rhetoric, but he was disappointed in his students. He said that they would rather be soldiers than scholars. Nevertheless he liked teaching and kept at it.

At some time while Basil was still in Athens, Gregory was married. This fact may explain his willingness to stay in Caesarea. Accounts of this marriage differ, but it seems probable that the young wife died and that Macrina urged Gregory to take up a career in the Church. At any rate, he did enter the ranks of the clergy and eventually became a priest and a preacher of considerable note. Gregory Nazianzen, who seemed to share with Basil the habit of criticizing and interfering with the younger Gregory, said of him rather unfairly, when he was teaching in the secular schools, that he would rather be an orator than a Christian. As a matter of fact, Gregory was a very good Christian, and there were many who said later that he was a greater philosopher and a more original thinker than either Basil or Gregory Nazianzen. He never had much chance to show his powers as long as those two famous scholars dominated the scene.

When Basil returned from Athens, it didn't take Macrina long to prick the bubble of his self-conceit and start him on a search for a better way of life. With all the children grown up now, Macrina had persuaded her mother to start a religious community for women. They chose as a site one of the family estates that lay along the river Iris because there was a church near by, and Macrina became the first superior of the colony. She managed it with the same skill that she had brought to the care of her large family. The nuns renounced all worldly goods, kept the canonical hours, rising at night to sing and pray, and labored hard to maintain the community and to care for the poor of the neighborhood.

Just when Basil's monastery was begun is not clear. Some accounts say that he started his first and then helped Macrina to organize hers. Others say that Macrina made the first move. In any case, the two colonies were established across the river from each other. Young Peter was Basil's first disciple, and Gregory was subjected to considerable pressure from Basil and Gregory Nazianzen to undertake a strict monastic life. He did try it, but he was not as strongly attracted to such an existence as the others and after a trial he gave it up.

While Gregory always deferred to Basil, he had certain ideas of his own. He couldn't help realizing that Basil was frequently a bit highhanded in his relationships with others, and at one time he actually took it upon himself to interfere. Basil had become bishop of Caesarea and one of his uncles, the one for whom

Gregory had been named, was opposed to him in some matter and there was a bitter quarrel. Gregory, who had Macrina's strong family sense, was ashamed of this division among relatives. He made some attempt at reconciliation, but succeeded only in offending everyone concerned. He never was very successful in diplomacy.

Although Basil recognized that his younger brother was decidedly gifted in his own way, he didn't give him credit for much practical sense. Nevertheless, he insisted upon appointing him bishop of Nyssa, an Arian-dominated town in lower Armenia. Basil was severely criticized for this move, chiefly because people thought that he should have given his brother a better appointment, but Basil had an answer: "It is better that my brother should do honor to the place than that the place should honor him."

Gregory was very reluctant to go, but, unlike Gregory Nazianzen who absolutely refused to go near the obscure place to which Basil assigned him, Gregory of Nyssa tried to make the best of things. He was too inexperienced, however, to be any match for the Arians in Nyssa. He wasn't a good administrator, he couldn't manage money, and he was easily deceived. The Arians accused him of embezzling church funds and had him imprisoned. Then they succeeded in having him deposed and sent into exile.

Meanwhile Emmelia died. Macrina was suffering from a protracted illness and longed to follow her mother. Peter, who was now a priest and superior of a neighboring monastery, was always a great comfort to Macrina, but she thought often of Gregory and followed his career with concern. It was eight years since he had visited his family and, stern as she was with herself, she yearned to see Gregory once again.

In the year 379 Basil died. Gregory, who had been recalled from exile, was on his way home from an important council of bishops in Antioch. It must have occurred somewhere near the time of Basil's death, for Gregory preached his brother's funeral sermon. Before returning to Nyssa he decided to visit Macrina and Peter. As he approached the monastery on the river Iris, the monks came out to meet him in a solemn ceremonial procession and led him to Macrina's monastery where he found the nuns all gathered in the church. There was no sign of Macrina, and Gregory learned that she was very ill. A nun led him to the barren little cell where she lived, and he found her lying on a board with a hollowed block for a pillow. Her only covering was a piece of haircloth. Gregory spent the day with her, and they talked as long-parted relatives will, of their parents, their brothers and sisters, their home life, and their school days. Macrina spoke so beautifully of Basil's death that Gregory later wrote a treatise based on her words. He called it "The Soul and the Resurrection."

In those days Vespers was called the "Prayer of the Lamp." At that hour Macrina sent Gregory to the church to pray. Early the next day when he went back to see her he knew that she was dying. She could not speak. Gregory signed her heart and mouth with the cross of Christ and gave her the last blessing. She had nothing in which to be buried but the patched habit she wore, so Gregory covered his sister with his bishop's cloak and took from her finger an iron ring which she had always worn, containing a relic of the True Cross. He gave it to the good nun who had cared for Macrina in her last illness.

Macrina's body was carried in procession to the church, followed by all the monks and nuns in two choirs, carrying lighted candles. Their voices were drowned out by the lamentations of the people who thronged about the bier of their benefactor.

Gregory preached Macrina's funeral sermon, as he had preached Basil's, and in telling about her life he mentioned certain early miracles known to all the household, but he refused to describe them "lest unbelievers scoff at the gifts of God." In a solemn burial service Macrina was placed beside her mother. Then Gregory knelt and kissed the earth that covered his mother and his heroic sister, who had been proclaimed a saint by the people even before she died.

When Gregory returned to his see in Nyssa after his long exile, the people welcomed him with joy, and now the quiet and self-effacing Gregory seemed to come into his own. He became a man of considerable influence. When Emperor Theodosius called the second general council at Constantinople, Gregory was given an important part in the proceedings, and he began to achieve a reputation as one of the mainstays of the Church.

Gregory's old skill at oratory had increased with the years, and he was often called upon to preach the panegyrics at the funerals, not only of church dignitaries, but of royalty, and it was he who delivered the discourse when Gregory Nazianzen was consecrated patriarch of Constantinople.

Letter-writing was another of Gregory's special accomplishments, and many interesting examples of his skill in this art still exist. The first time he saw Constantinople, he wrote letters to his family describing that city of wonders sitting on its seven hills surrounded by the shining waters of the Bosporus, the Sea of Marmora, the Black Sea, and the Golden Horn, and with its harbor bright with the gay pennons of the world's shipping.

Constantinople, Gregory told them, was the crossroads of the world, teeming with merchants, travelers, pilgrims, monks, priests, and peddlers. He told of the Hippodrome and the chariot races, of trained dogs, clowns, and jugglers, and of the arrogant ladies who were carried through the streets with slaves holding parasols and canopies over their heads. Everything was on a magnificent scale—the paved streets and broad avenues; the palaces, churches, and theaters with their porticoes, their graceful arches, and their domes of polished copper; the public baths and the aqueducts; the fantastic pavilions, cupolas, and shining minarets; and the handsome private houses. Emperor Constantine had brought treasures from all over the world to enrich his capital city.

There were so many things to see that even an accomplished letter-writer like Gregory found it hard to describe them. He noted the crowded streets, the bazaars with their sellers of silks and perfumes, the sheep and cattle markets, the miserable slums, and in contrast the golden chariots of the rich and the imperial purple everywhere.

The "city guarded by God" was filled with

holy relics. There were two pieces of the True Cross, the head of the lance that pierced the Savior's side, two of the nails used in the Crucifixion, and other authentic relics. To Gregory, the most beautiful thing in the city was the glorious cathedral of St. Sophia, also known as *Hagia Sophia*, which means "holy wisdom." (It was there that he preached at Gregory Nazianzen's consecration.) St. Sophia was a forerunner of what we know as Byzantine architecture, with its great center dome and four half-domes, its brightly colored tiles and shining gilt crosses, its richly sculptured walls, and its four slender turrets. The interior was splendid beyond belief with cedar, ivory, and amber, jasper, porphyry, marble, and alabaster. There were silver lamps and golden crosses, glass inlaid with agate and ivory, glistening mosaics, priceless illuminated manuscripts, rich embroideries, and the books of the Gospels bound in gold. Thousands of skillful hands had built the cathedral of the Holy Wisdom.

The Byzantine people spoke Greek, but they always thought of themselves as Romans, and Gregory noticed that the citizens of Constantinople were much given to talk and argument.

"Everyone wants to argue about religion," wrote Gregory. "The money-changers, the bakers, the very slaves in the public baths will argue with anyone who will answer. I am beginning to think that everyone in Constantinople is a doctor of theology. There is not a man in the city who cannot preach a pretty good sermon. Anyone who waits on you in a shop or just happens to be standing on a street corner can defend his Christian beliefs like a Father of the Church."

In his later years Gregory did quite a bit of traveling and made crisp comment on what he saw. When he visited Palestine he was very much shocked at the manner in which pilgrimages were conducted. So many abuses did he observe that he wrote a treatise on the subject in which he said sharply that pilgrimages, as they were being carried on, were not a devotion to be recommended. He added that they were no part of the gospel precept and that so far as he himself was concerned he derived no benefit from visiting the Holy Places.

St. Gregory of Nyssa died some time between 394 and 400. (Even the date of his death is not certain.) He is remembered as a man of great eloquence and a strong voice against heresy. He was virtuous and well-intentioned but possessed of little worldly wisdom, and his appointment to the see of Nyssa was an error in judgment on the part of his brother Basil. Some of his most important work consisted of treatises on the Holy Trinity, the immortality of the soul, and such themes. He wrote a life of Moses, a very good catechism, and many excellent sermons. He said of himself that he had been buffeted about "like a piece of wood in the water," but reading his life, one is impressed by the fact that he was a man of peace, that he bore no resentment toward those who gave him bad advice or ordered him to do things against his will, and that when any of his friends or his family needed him he was always there. Gregory of Nyssa was not the least important member of his distinguished family.

CHAPTER NINE

St. Cyril of Jerusalem

The Greek name Cyril means "little lord," but it is unlikely that St. Cyril of Jerusalem was of the nobility. Very little is known of his early life except that he was born in or near Jerusalem, was brought up there as a Christian, and received a good general education. He must have spent considerable time in the study of the Scriptures, since he became famous for his catechetical instructions and was made a Doctor of the Church because of his outstanding reputation as a theologian. He served as a deacon for ten years in the Church of Jerusalem and was ordained a priest in the year 345.

The fourth century was one of great struggle and great growth for the Church. In the year 345, about mid-century, the pro-Arian Constantius II was eastern emperor and St. Julius I was the Pope of Rome. St. Paul the Hermit had been dead only three years; St. Antony of Egypt was well over ninety and waiting for God to call him, though he would have to wait ten years longer; St. Hilarion had organized the cloisters and lauras all over Syria and Palestine and was living near the city of Gaza, not far south of Jerusalem; and St. Pachomius was still ruling his abbey at Tabenna in upper Egypt. St. Athanasius was leading a hunted life as patriarch of Alexandria; St. Basil the Great, St. Gregory Nazianzen, and St. Gregory of Nyssa, who would soon take the torch of faith from his hands, were not yet even baptized; and in the ancient city of Jerusalem a quiet, scholarly, and virtuous young priest named Cyril had just been assigned to the task of instructing the catechumens.

In those days it was not easy to become a Christian. Adult catechumens had to go through a long and serious preparation. Among them were Jews, pagans, and adult children of Christian parents. The course of instruction was divided into various units climaxed by solemn rites during Lent and Holy Week. During the usual course of instruction, catechumens learned the rudiments of the faith, but the great mysteries of the Holy Eucharist and the Real Presence were never disclosed until after baptism. Those already instructed persons, of whom there were many, who preferred to remain catechumens in order to avoid the serious duties and responsibilities of the professed Christians, were known as Competents. They were allowed to attend the first part of the Liturgy, but were dismissed by the deacon before the Offertory.

At a point about halfway through Lent, the catechumens were taught the Creed and the Our Father. Later on they were anointed with the "oil of catechumens" and made their profession of faith. During the Easter Vigil, right after the reading of the prophecies, the bishop blessed the baptismal font. The font was really a large pool, and as the catechumens descended into it one by one they were baptized by a triple immersion, after which they were confirmed with chrism. When they came out of the font they were robed in new white garments and each one was given a burning light.

Now they were known as the Illuminati, or enlightened ones, and were finally taught the last mystery, that of the Holy Eucharist.

The Illuminati wore their white robes all during Easter week. On Low Sunday they received Holy Communion for the first time and were then known as the Faithful unless they had committed some serious sin. Such unfortunates were called Penitents. The Eastern Church still baptizes by immersion, but all the steps of the ancient ceremony are present in condensed form in the rite used in the Western Church.

The work that Cyril was assigned to do was that of instructing the Competents and the Enlightened Ones. For this purpose he devised a course of instruction in the faith so complete and orderly that it remained the standard system for many centuries. Cyril never used a book when he was instructing catechumens. He talked to them freely and informally and held their attention by little human interest stories about the first disciples and their families, the Apostles, and other characters mentioned in the Scriptures. He liked to dwell on details such as the stone that sealed the Savior's tomb or the lance the centurion bore. He was always thoughtful and sympathetic in his contacts with his pupils, shortening his discourse, for example, when his hearers had been fasting long and in many ways looking after their comfort.

At various times Cyril of Jerusalem was accused of being in sympathy with the Arians. Priests or bishops who tried to get along with the Arians without open warfare were often so accused. Others who went a little too far in conciliation were known as semi-Arians, but Cyril was never accused of teaching false doctrine. He taught the true Nicene Creed and placed great emphasis upon the doctrine of the Real Presence and upon transubstantiation. Over and over again he impressed upon the catechumens that when they received Holy Communion they became of one Body and one Blood with Christ, and he urged them to think of themselves as Christ-bearers.

In the year 350 Cyril was elected bishop of Jerusalem. During the first year of his reign several miracles occurred that made a great impression on the public. One of these, which was witnessed by hundreds of onlookers, occurred on a fine morning in May. There appeared in the heavens a great luminous cross just over Golgotha and extending as far as Mount Olivet. Nearly everyone in the city saw it and declared that it was no natural phenomenon or trick of vision. It remained in position for several hours and shone brighter than the sun. Crowds of people ran to the church and gave praise to God for this sign of His glory. Many believed that the miracle was an evidence of God's approval of Bishop Cyril who was beloved of his people.

But Cyril's immediate superior, Acacius, the metropolitan of Caesarea (the Roman capital of Palestine), did not love Cyril or approve of him. Acacius was a semi-Arian, an ambitious and envious man. He resented Cyril's popularity and determined to get rid of him. The see of Jerusalem had always been independent, but Acacius now claimed jurisdiction over it because it was within the bounds of the church of Caesarea. Cyril said that Jerusalem was an "apostolic throne" and subject to no superior. Acacius knew that he could get support from Arians and semi-Arians, so he called a council at Caesarea. Cyril refused to go. The Arian bishops then drew up a list of charges against him. They said that he had been guilty of selling church property. This was true. He had sold unnecessary vestments and sacred vessels to get food for the poor during a time of famine. But many other bishops, famous ones, too, had done the same thing in similar situations. Another charge, made by Acacius, was that he was guilty of insubordination. There were not enough non-Arian bishops at the synod to save Cyril, and he was banished from Jerusalem.

Cyril took refuge with a hospitable semi-Arian bishop named Silvanus and made several attempts to secure reinstatement, but it was almost two years later that the council of Seleucia was called. Nearly all the bishops at this council were either Arian or semi-Arian, and all of them came from Egypt. Cyril attended this time and sat among the semi-Arians with his host Silvanus. Acacius was very angry at Cyril's presence. The minute he saw him he stalked out of the council room, but he returned later in a very bad temper. In due course the bishops considered Cyril's case, and after considerable debate he was vindicated and the charges against him dismissed. He was reinstated as bishop of Jerusalem and this time it was Acacius who was deposed. In those days being a bishop on either side was a hazardous occupation.

For a little while Cyril presided over his see in peace, but Acacius was not without further resources. He went to Emperor Constantius and again accused Cyril of having misused church property. This time, however, he decided to make the charge one of personal interest to the emperor so that he would take immediate action. He told Constantius that Cyril had sold a gold-brocaded baptismal vestment that had been presented by Constantine the Great to Bishop Macarius. To make his story still more convincing, Acacius added that the vestment had been seen on a comedian acting in a cheap theater. Quite naturally the emperor was indignant. Apparently it didn't occur to him to doubt the word of Acacius. In any case, Cyril was banished again.

Emperor Constantius died in 361 and was succeeded by Julian the Apostate. It does seem as if the first thing each emperor did was to reverse all the decrees of the one who had preceded him. This habit worked out well for Cyril, however, for Julian proclaimed the restoration of all bishops deposed by Constantius. Back went Cyril to Jerusalem and back went Athanasius to Alexandria. Athanasius was already well accustomed to the life of an exile, but Cyril was not yet so experienced.

Julian was a better student of human nature than some of the other emperors. He knew better than to make martyrs of these Christians. The more martyrs, the more Christians, he had observed. He had a better plan. He would do everything in his power to discredit the Christian religion and the name of Christ. It was his aim to destroy Christianity entirely and restore the old gods and idols. He hated all Jews, but he thought he saw a way of using them to defeat the Christians. Christ had foretold the destruction of Jerusalem. Therefore if he could make that prophecy false, the whole Christian belief would collapse.

The emperor gave huge sums of money to the Jewish people for the restoration of the temple, and the work was begun with vigor, but Cyril and his people were not disturbed. They believed in the word of Christ, and Cyril assured his flock that in the end the project would fail, no matter how well it was begun. Some of the weaker in faith may have had their moments of doubt, but just as Cyril had prophesied, the work had to be abandoned. Fires, earthquakes, the collapse of roofs and walls, and other disasters forced the builders to give up their efforts. Some historians have cast doubts upon the interference of natural phenomena, but such reliable writers as St. Ambrose and St. John Chrysostom recorded them as truth. Whatever the reason, the temple was not rebuilt, and Julian's scheme failed.

When Emperor Julian died in 363 he was succeeded by Jovian, whose reign lasted only a year, and then by Valentinian who took over the Western empire and appointed his brother Valens as his caesar, or assistant, in the East. Valens was an Arian of the most extreme type. It was he whom St. Basil the Great was to oppose so courageously. He immediately banished all the bishops who had been restored by Julian. This was Cyril's third exile and it lasted for eleven years. Then Valens was succeeded in the West by the Catholic emperor Gratian and in the East by the first Catholic emperor ever to reign over the Eastern empire, Theodosius the Great.

One of the first acts of Theodosius was to recall all the bishops exiled by Valens. When Cyril got back to his see in Jerusalem he found the city beset by heresies, schisms, and crimes of all kinds. He reported the state of affairs to the council of Catholic bishops then meeting in Antioch, and they appointed Gregory of Nyssa, who was also returning from exile and had attended the council, to go to Jerusalem on his way home and see what advice he could give. He found conditions pretty bad himself, and it was after this visit that he wrote his famous treatise on pilgrimages. Going on a so-called pilgrimage to visit the Holy Places had become the fashionable thing to do, and the behavior of the "pilgrims" was often far from edifying. Cyril must have managed to make some improvements, however, because St. Basil in one of his many letters mentioned the fact that the diocese of Jerusalem had flourished under Cyril. Considering the fact that Cyril was a bishop for thirty-five years and that he spent sixteen of them in exile, he probably did as well as anyone could do.

Theodosius now began a strong campaign

against paganism. He closed all the temples and forbade the private practice of pagan cults. He proclaimed the whole empire Christian and made Christianity the law of the land. Church feast days were celebrated as public holidays, and the bishops became officers of the state. The Eastern empire began to regard the emperor as the supreme leader of both Church and State. He was almost like a god. With Church and State practically one and the whole governed by the emperor, what need was there for a pope? The seeds of separation sown back in the time of Constantine the Great, were growing up into a hedge between the East and West, and to this day one of the thorniest problems with which the Church is plagued is that of the separation of Church and State.

Under Theodosius, the Arian heresy was subdued completely so far as state approval was concerned, but the emperor felt that the whole Eastern Church needed to be reorganized and many principles of doctrine and practice reaffirmed. He therefore called the second ecumenical council to convene in Constantinople in the year 381. To this council went Cyril who took his place as patriarch of Jerusalem, equal with those of Alexandria and Antioch. This was verily a council of saints with St. Meletius, St. Gregory Nazianzen, and St. Gregory of Nyssa present, and St. Cyril, too, but curiously enough it was not a true ecumenical council. All the bishops of the empire had been invited, but only 150 came. There were no Latin delegates and no legates from Rome. Later on, however, the proceedings were ratified by the Holy See, and it was numbered in the list of true ecumenical synods. One of the decisions that was very important to Cyril was the declaration that his consecration as bishop of Jerusalem in 350 had been valid and canonical.

St. Cyril of Jerusalem died in the year 386, and on his feast day, which is March eighteenth, the Church takes special pains to clear his name of any error:

> *At Jerusalem, St. Cyril, Bishop, who having suffered many injuries from the Arians for the faith, and having been many times driven from his see, at last rested in peace, illustrious with the glory of holiness; of whose untarnished faith the second ecumenical synod, writing to Damasus, gave a splendid witness.*

CHAPTER TEN

St. John Chrysostom

If ever there was a controversial figure it was John Chrysostom. No one seemed to be neutral about him. Unjust rulers and worldly ecclesiastics hated and feared him. The common people loved him. He was called the "golden-tongued" because of his marvelous eloquence, but there was nothing golden about the tongue-lashings he administered to sinners and heretics, to lax clergy and luxury-loving women. They all had good cause to fear him.

John Chrysostom was short in stature, with arms and legs so thin that he looked like a spider. He had a pointed chin with a short beard, and his cheeks were pale and sunken. Because he had a natural tendency to like fine wines, costly foods, and worldly pleasures, he put himself under such severe discipline that he spent most of his life in physical misery. He had fasted so much that the slightest excess of food gave him headaches and sharp stomach pains. Even when he was a famous bishop, he never dined with anyone else or invited guests to his palace. (He had sold nearly all the furnishings anyway and kept the most meager household.) Many people, of course, were offended, but he paid no attention. Some people said he was a saint and others that he was a meddling, troublesome, domineering prelate. John always either inspired great affection and loyalty or kindled strong resentment, and he didn't care which.

This remarkable man, considered the greatest pulpit orator of all time, one of the three Holy Hierarchs of the Eastern Church, reformer, liturgist, and Doctor of the Church, was born in the proud city of Antioch in Syria, third city of the Roman Empire, and the chief center of Greek culture in Asia. It was a rich, pleasure-loving city of luxury and amusement. John's parents were wealthy and distinguished. His father died when John was very young, but his mother saw to it that he had a good classical education, with law in mind as a career. He was a brilliant success as a student, and he loved the forum, the theater, and the schools; but after he met St. Meletius, Archbishop of Antioch, nothing but the Christian faith interested him. He was baptized and decided to become a monk.

His mother wept and scolded and accused him of leaving her, a poor widow, all alone. Her methods worked. John stayed, but he lived as much like a monk as possible. After his mother's death he lived for six years with a colony of monks and for two years as a solitary, but his health broke down from too much austerity and he was finally persuaded to return to Antioch and become a priest. He was ordained in the year 386 and made a bishop in 391. Although he felt himself unworthy of his great office, he set himself the task of becoming a good priest. Old Archbishop Flavian, who had ordained him, did not like to preach, so he turned over most of that work to his new assistant, and the young man took the job seriously.

John went after the Christians hammer and tongs. He laid down the law to those who thought of nothing but wealth and public office and to the rich who encouraged strife and litigation. He preached against dishonest dealings, false oaths, extortion, usury, and profanity, and he hit hard at the smug and pious:

"Heaven," he thundered at them, "is for those who do positive good, not for those who merely abstain from sin."

He kept after those who had wealth, not because he opposed riches, if they were used rightly. It was "tainted money" that he detested, money that came from cheating workmen, charging high interest rates, and indulging in irresponsible luxury. He reproached the people for vanity and self-love:

"Your chief concern as you walk through public places is that you should not soil your boots with mud or dust, but you let your soul grovel while you care for your boots. Boots are made to be soiled. If you can't bear it, take them off and wear them on your head. You laugh at that, but I weep for your folly."

John's sermons and treatises were filled with wisdom and practical common sense. He said that a good Christian life was not just for monks but for everybody. He urged strong family life, warned young people against marrying for money, and deplored worldly education. He wanted boys and young men guarded as carefully as girls. He preached against charms, magic, fortunetellers, astrology, and all kinds of superstition, against pompous funerals, and the use of black for mourning. Constantly he exhorted the people to be orderly as they came to Communion and not to crowd or push each other when approaching the Lord's table. Any one of his sermons could be read from a pulpit today, and it would sound just as appropriate as on the day he delivered it.

Antioch was a worldly city. The people had to be taught to pray. "Prayer," said John, "must be a raising of the heart and mind to God, not just asking for something." He believed that private prayer was good, but that public prayer was even more important. He wanted "an assembly of the faithful wherein the cry of the worshipers goes up with one accord, where the clergy preside and unite the weaker and the stronger supplications into one great prayer to heaven." And to this day, in the Eastern rites, there is fervent participation of both people and clergy in the Divine Liturgy.

John believed in returning thanks for favors received. One day when heavy rains had done much damage, he organized a procession with prayers and hymns to ask for help. The rain stopped. It was Good Friday and the people should have been preparing for the Easter

Vigil, but as soon as the rain ceased many of them dashed off to the races. John was furious.

"Think shame to yourselves," he said with withering scorn. "With all creation ministering to your needs, you run after the devil's pleasures."

He wanted the congregation to listen when he preached.

"Inattention," said John to his flock, "is disgraceful. When an imperial decree is read, you do not dare to speak or move lest you be charged with sedition. But you are not afraid of incurring a greater danger by showing disrespect to the word of God."

Once he scolded his hearers because they were watching the lamp-lighters instead of attending to him. "I, too, am lighting a lamp," said he, "the lamp of God."

Some of John Chrysostom's most eloquent sermons were pleas for Christian charity. He preached against slavery and tried to better the condition of slaves, urging the churches to purchase serfs and free them. "The world," he said, "is like a household wherein all the servants should receive equal allowances because all men are equal, since they are brothers."

There were good reasons for John's extraordinary popularity as a preacher. In spite of his insignificant appearance, he really had great charm and eloquence, but it was his good common sense and understanding of human nature that endeared him to the people. He knew their problems and their temptations, and while he scolded them for their weaknesses he gave them simple, down-to-earth lessons in practical living and kept pulling them up toward God by the sheer force of his character.

John's popularity with the common people was unquestioned, but the clergy and the ruling classes had no love for him. In 398, Emperor Arcadius made him patriarch of Constantinople, not because he liked him, but because he thought that John's prestige might be useful to him. John did not want to leave Antioch. Moreover, he had to be practically kidnapped because the people grieved so much at his going. They jammed the church at his last sermon, and he came out and sat in the midst of them.

Things went badly from the first in Constantinople. (Someone once said of John that the only way to keep him out of trouble would be to deprive him of speech.) He began immediately to reprimand the clergy for laxity, the monks for leaving their monasteries and roaming the streets, and the magistrates, officials, and court favorites for servility and immorality. Worst of all, he preached a particularly outspoken sermon on the worldliness and frivolity of the court and especially the foolishness of fashionable women. The Empress Eudoxia was outraged. She took the whole thing personally, as well she might, for it was directed at her. Eudoxia became John's bitter enemy.

At the same time John was making other enemies among the clergy. Those who enjoyed luxury resented John's meager diet and lack of hospitality. ("I'll season his soup for him!" said one.) Others opposed him in matters of doctrine and practice. The best of the clergy were on his side, but there were many against him. A certain worldly and ambitious bishop named Theophilus found it to his advantage to stir up trouble by accusing John of teaching false doctrine.

The charges made by Theophilus were based on a controversy which had been going on since the third century when the teachings of a monk named Origen attracted many followers. He was a saintly man and a brilliantly original thinker, but his theology, which lent itself to a great variety of interpretation, dominated the Eastern Church for over two hundred years and became the source of much error and many bitter arguments.

The great Christian centers disagreed about Origen. The Alexandrians, including most of the Egyptian monks, accepted him completely;

the Church of Antioch rejected him; and the Cappadocians stood midway between. Athanasius, Basil, Gregory Nazianzen, and Gregory of Nyssa admired much of Origen's thinking but rejected his errors. John Chrysostom was of the school of Antioch—literal, rational, and unaffected by literary grace or eloquence. When he preached he gave no quarter. Theophilus wanted to get rid of him, so he managed to get a civil order to expel the "disorderly monks" from Egypt. Soldiers were sent, the monks driven out, their monasteries burned, and they themselves dispersed. Some of them came to Constantinople to appeal to the emperor and the patriarch. John Chrysostom gave them shelter. That gave Theophilus a chance to say that John was in sympathy with the teachings of Origen. The battle was on.

Theophilus already had Eudoxia to back him up. Now he enlisted the help of twenty-nine bishops, all of whom were annoyed at John for one reason or another. They pretended to call a council or synod and asked John to preside. He knew better than to accept. Next they summoned him to answer the charges made against him. John said that he would not appear except before a properly constituted and just tribunal. Then they deposed him for failing to appear, and he was banished to a small village on the Asiatic side of the Black Sea.

The people of Constantinople were so infuriated that the palace was alarmed, especially since an earthquake occurred just then. Eudoxia was superstitious. She had John recalled. He refused to come, but they brought him by force. Theophilus left the city, but neither he nor the empress had given up. Eudoxia had a silver statue of herself placed on a column in the square right in front of the cathedral of St. Sophia. There was a noisy, disorderly crowd singing and dancing at the unveiling, and John preached a powerful sermon against the scandal.

All winter the battle went on. The people guarded their bishop day and night. At Christmas the emperor would not attend the Liturgy in the cathedral. At Eastertime, when the cathedral was crowded with worshipers and neophytes awaiting baptism, soldiers were sent in. They dispersed the people, injuring many, and desecrated the altar. "The scattered sheep," said John, "kept Easter in the woods." Pope Innocent tried to intervene, but John's enemies said there would be no peace in Constantinople as long as John was there.

At last Emperor Arcadius signed another order of exile, and once more John Chrysostom was shipped off by boat, this time to the Taurus Mountains. Fearful disorders followed. The people were violently aroused, and there was fierce fighting. All worship was forbidden, and many martyrs died for their faith. Arcadius continued the persecution mercilessly, and the condition of the Church in Constantinople grew steadily worse.

John was now nearly sixty, and the ten-week journey on mule-back to the lonely mountain village in Cappadocia was very hard on him. The climate was harsh and conditions primitive. Nevertheless during the three years he stayed there he wrote hundreds of brilliant, persuasive letters to bishops, priests, deacons, monks, soldiers, consuls, and ladies of the nobility. Considering the difficulties in delivering the letters, it is astonishing that so many of them survived, but two or three faithful messengers made the long dangerous journey whenever the roads were passable.

It was bitter cold in winter, and John suffered headaches, sleeplessness, and severe stomach troubles. If he tried to make a fire for warmth, the smoke hurt his throat and lungs. Still the spidery little man survived, and the emperor grew increasingly angry at the influence he was able to wield from such a distance. He ordered John sent to a still more distant place on the Black Sea. The soldiers had orders to treat him so badly that he would never get there, so they hurried him along without mercy.

One day he could go no farther, and they stopped at the little chapel of St. Basilicus. The martyred saint appeared to John that night and told him that his trials were at an end. In the morning John asked for a priest to bring him Communion. Then he said quietly, "Glory be to God for all things," and the golden tongue was still. They buried him there in the tomb of St. Basilicus.

In our admiration for St. John Chrysostom's remarkable gifts as a writer and orator, we sometimes tend to forget his contributions to the reform of Church music. In the Eastern Church, the word *Liturgy* is used instead of our *Mass*. The Byzantine Liturgy is a beautiful service, enhanced by richly embroidered vestments, flowers, lights, and incense, jeweled vessels, glorious music, and colorful processions. John Chrysostom shortened the Liturgy of St. Basil, which had already been abbreviated from the very long and ancient Liturgy of St. James, and one authority has said of this work: "The Greek Liturgy of St. John Chrysostom is one of the most beautiful expressions of Christian piety in the world."

Thirty years after the death of John Chrysostom, Emperor Theodosius II had his relics brought back to Constantinople. In the presence of vast throngs, he laid his face upon John's coffin and prayed that his parents might be forgiven for their persecution of a great saint. And today the Byzantine Church still sings of him:

The holy church rejoices mystically at the return of your sacred relics; she never ceases teaching her children to sing of you and of the grace that comes through your prayers, O John of the Golden Tongue.

CHAPTER ELEVEN

St. Nicholas of Myra

Among the bishops who attended the first ecumenical council in 325 was a quiet man named Nicholas. He made no particular impression on the assemblage. (One writer, it is true, asserts that he slapped the heretic Arius in the face, but that seems almost too much to believe.) He had been summoned from his see in Asia Minor by Emperor Constantine and sat with the others listening to the eloquence of a young deacon named Athanasius. He cast his votes when the time came to do so, signed his name to the new Creed, and eventually went home more or less unnoticed. But that self-same bishop became one of the most famous saints in the world, the dearly loved St. Nicholas, patron saint of children, and a highly revered figure in the Eastern Church, where his feast day is celebrated on December 6.

Most of the historians maintain that there are practically no solemnly attested facts known about St. Nicholas, but they have to admit that there is a great body of oral tradition enshrined in the hearts of the people and that in it, as in all legend, there must be a good deal of truth. St. Nicholas, according to tradition, was born in the little village of Para in Lycia, Asia Minor, near the beginning of the fourth century. His father's name was Epiphanius and his mother's Joanna. They belonged to a small group of Christians living in a pagan community. Over two hundred years earlier the apostle Paul had come from his far land to tell the people about Christ. Kings and emperors had come and gone since that time. There had been cruel persecutions and many had died for their faith, but the Christians of Para never forgot. Whenever a child was born he was signed with the sign of the Cross in the presence of the people, who asked God to make him a good Christian, strong in the faith. Epiphanius and Joanna were not disappointed in their son. At a very early age he understood the Christian teaching. He kept the Church laws faithfully and soon attracted the attention of the neighbors, who began to call him a holy child.

The family of young Nicholas was very rich. They had olive groves and vineyards, a fine large house, and many servants; but they lived as good Christians, kind to the less fortunate and generous in the service of the Church. They died when Nicholas was quite young, however, and as soon as the boy found himself possessed of so much wealth, he began to give it away. His relatives were disturbed.

"If you don't keep some of your property for yourself," they said, "how do you expect to live?"

"I have more than I need," said Nicholas. "It makes me feel happy when I see hungry people eating good nourishing food or when I see a cloak of mine on a ragged child."

When he grew a little older, Nicholas decided that he would like to be a monk. He studied the Scriptures diligently and served the poor as well as he could until he was old enough to go and live in one of the communities that were beginning to crowd the desert places. There he lived a happy, orderly life, working in the fields or vineyards all day and rising in the night to sing God's praises. His food was coarse, black bread and cheese with a few green vegetables and a cup of water, and he slept on the ground or on a hard wooden plank with one thin blanket for summer and winter.

In those days it was the dream of every monk to make a pilgrimage to the Holy Land. Monks didn't travel like the fashionable pilgrims whom St. Gregory of Nyssa criticized so severely. They made the long journey barefoot, with a few crusts of bread in a leather pouch, a goatskin bag for water, and a heavy staff to help them climb the stony hills and ford the rushing waters. Nicholas was too humble to ask permission to go, but the thought was often in his mind. Then quite suddenly, his dream came true, and he found himself setting out for Egypt where, like everyone else, he hoped to visit St. Antony. Then he would go to Palestine and the Holy Places.

Travel by land was slow and difficult, but travel by sea was far worse. As Nicholas boarded a small and clumsy boat for part of his journey, the sky and sea seemed peaceful enough, but Nicholas looked at the captain.

"A storm will be upon us soon," he said. "It will be better not to sail just yet."

The captain laughed and so did the sailors.

"Stick to your prayers, holy one," said the captain, "and I'll navigate the ship."

When the ship was well out at sea, a violent tempest arose. Fearful winds tossed the boat about like a cork. The terrified passengers blamed the captain for starting, but Nicholas knelt on the deck and asked Christ Who had walked on the waves to control them now and save the ship from destruction. In a moment the winds and the sea became quiet and so did the captain. He was too astonished to speak, but the sailors whispered to each other, "This man must be a saint."

Nicholas would have liked to stay in the Holy Land and live there as a solitary, but in a dream God told him that he must go back to his own monastery. He seems to have been rather unfortunate in his choice of ships, for the captain of the one he boarded for his return journey was a really wicked man. He had planned to sell Nicholas and some of the other passengers into slavery, but luckily there were sailors aboard who had been part of the crew on the ship that Nicholas saved from the tempest. They had not forgotten him.

"Be on your guard, good brother," they said. "The captain is not going to stop at your port. He will take you to a slave port and sell you."

Nicholas thanked the loyal sailors and again

he asked God to help him. This time he really wanted a storm, and God sent one so fierce that the captain could not control his ship at all. It was blown straight into the harbor where Nicholas wanted to go.

When Nicholas again reached his monastery he found that the abbot had died and that his fellow monks were waiting to make him abbot. He didn't want to be an abbot, but he had no choice. He bowed to the will of God and ruled the monastery wisely and well. When the bishop of Myra died, a council of bishops met to elect his successor. The presiding bishop was told by a messenger in a dream to stand at the door of the church in the morning and to consecrate as bishop the first man to enter. The heavenly messenger added that the man's name would be Nicholas.

In the morning the bishop was at his post, and along came Nicholas bright and early to say his morning Mass. The bishop asked his name.

"Nicholas, servant of your lordship," answered Nicholas humbly.

So Nicholas, again protesting, was made bishop of Myra. He much preferred his patched monk's robe and pilgrim staff to the jeweled vestments and gilded crosier, but he did his best as usual and is said to have been humble, grave, and prayerful, a persuasive speaker, and a kindly counselor. It was during this time that he attended the ecumenical council at Nicaea and, we hardly dare to hope, gave the heretic Arius a piece of his mind.

Nicholas loved his people, especially the children, and he could not bear to see them suffer. Once when a severe famine plagued the city of Myra, Nicholas looked at the great shiploads of grain being sent to the emperor's already-overflowing granaries. He begged the overseers to give him some for his people. The officers were afraid.

"Our cargo is weighed and measured at Alexandria," they told him. "We must deliver exactly that weight and that measure to the emperor's overseers."

"Do as I ask you," pleaded Nicholas, "and I promise that the imperial customs officers will not find a grain less than that with which you began your journey."

The overseers believed him. Nicholas gave the grain to the poor, and it multiplied so miraculously that it lasted for two years with enough left over for sowing. Moreover, the emperor's shipment was not the less by a single grain.

Nicholas did more than help himself to the emperor's grain. He actually reproved the ruler for injustice. It happened this way. Three innocent officers had been condemned to death by the consul in Myra. St. Nicholas rescued the men and was very indignant at the consul, but forgave him when the three victims interceded for him. It happened that three princes who were on the emperor's business in Myra were witnesses of the whole affair, and it made a great impression on them. Not long after their return to Constantinople, certain jealous courtiers poisoned the emperor's mind against them and they, too, were thrown into prison. During the night one of the men recalled how Bishop Nicholas had saved the three innocent officers in Myra and they began to pray most earnestly to the good bishop. That same night while Emperor Constantine was sleeping peacefully, Nicholas appeared to him and told him that the three princes were innocent. Constantine was understandably astonished and not very well pleased.

"Who are you," he asked, "who dare to enter my apartment at night and speak in this manner?"

"I am Nicholas, bishop of Myra," was the reply, and the bishop proceeded to scold the emperor right heartily for his lack of justice.

Nicholas also visited the prefect who had ordered the executions. The emperor and the prefect exchanged experiences in the morning. They sent for the three princes.

"Do you know a man named Nicholas?"

They did, indeed, and they told Constantine all about him. The emperor was much impressed, too. He sent gifts to Bishop Nicholas together with a request for his prayers, and the three princes became Christians.

One of the most popular tales about St. Nicholas is that of the three girls who were very sad because their father was too poor to provide dowries for them. One night as they were discussing their misfortunes in their cold, cheerless room, there came flying through the broken window pane a purse of gold. One hundred golden coins! They counted them over and over. With that treasure, it was naturally not difficult to secure a suitable husband for the oldest girl. The same thing happened with the second daughter, but when it came the turn of the youngest girl she caught Bishop Nicholas before he could get away. Every year after that she baked triple-kneaded cakes and gave them to the poor on the sixth of December (now the bishop's feast day) and in many places such cakes are still baked in honor of St. Nicholas.

When at last the good Bishop Nicholas died, there was great mourning. He was buried in the cathedral at Myra, and for hundreds of years his tomb was a place of pilgrimage. But when Myra was besieged by the Saracens the city was practically destroyed and all the beautiful objects in the cathedral were stolen. The priests managed, however, to hide their greatest treasure, the relics of St. Nicholas. Not long afterward, some merchants in the city of Bari in Italy, who had been helped by praying to St. Nicholas, agreed that his bones should not be allowed to remain among pagans and infidels. They decided to bring his body to Bari.

In the year 1087 they voyaged to Myra, searched among the ruins of the old cathedral, and to their great joy found the casket in which Nicholas had been buried. They carried it back with them in triumph and built the beautiful Church of San Nicolo to do him honor. Many of the kings of Sicily were crowned in that church, and St. Nicholas wrought many miracles there. One strange phenomenon which is said to exist even now is that of the miraculous myrrh or balm, a sweet-smelling substance exuded from the body of St. Nicholas and known as the "manna of St. Nicholas."

Probably the most faithful of all the followers of St. Nicholas are the sailors. They still observe a special feast day in his honor at which time they carry the statue of San Nicolo from the cathedral down to the harbor and take it aboard a gaily decorated boat. Then they sail out to sea, praying St. Nicholas to give them prosperous voyages and favorable winds.

At night the statue is returned to its place in a colorful procession which goes singing and marching through gaily decorated streets with fireworks as a climax. On certain days pilgrims come in thousands, making the circle of the church on their knees, and when they leave, each one receives from a priest a tiny bottle containing some of the "manna of St. Nicholas."

The fame of St. Nicholas spread from Italy and Greece to nearly all parts of the world. Thousands and thousands of churches have been named in his honor. In the Middle Ages, there were four hundred churches bearing his name in England alone. He is said to have been represented in art more frequently than any other of the saints except Our Lady. More churches were named throughout the world for St. Nicholas than for any one of the apostles, and his name appears in the Litany of the Saints.

St. Nicholas is the patron saint of sailors, merchants, bakers, bankers, travelers, brewers, coopers, pawnbrokers, and, of all things, robbers! He became, of course, the special saint of children, and there are few countries where he is not known under one name or another. He is the patron saint of Greece, Sicily, Galway, and many other countries and provinces, but curiously enough, in the old days it was always Russia that loved him best. The Russian winter was supposed to begin on the feast of St. Nicholas, and at the end of the Nicholastide came the great event of the blessing of the waters. Even the Czar and the Czarina were there.

In the Byzantine liturgy, in one of the long prayers in honor of the Blessed Virgin, the prophets, Apostles, and others, occurs this passage:

> *Of our holy fathers and saints: Basil the Great, Gregory the Theologian, and John the Gold-mouthed, Athanasius and Cyril, Nicholas of Myra, Cyril and Methodius, teachers of the Slavs, the holy martyr Josaphat, and all the saintly prelates. . . .*

So there is good St. Nicholas, friend of the children, honored among the greatest.

CHAPTER TWELVE

Simeon Stylites

St. Simeon Stylites lived for thirty-seven years on a platform about six feet in diameter, with no roof and not even a seat, on top of a pillar which, at the last, was eighty feet high. It is hard to know what to say about Simeon. In these days, psychiatrists would probably call him an exhibitionist. In his own day there were many who laughed at him, others who were violently opposed to him, and still others who came to laugh and stayed to pray. But to Simeon his life was his vocation, and his frequently exasperated superiors finally came to agree with him. He preached twice a day from his lofty height and made a great impression on the people, particularly on barbarians and infidels. He was responsible for hundreds of conversions and countless miracles and was consulted by princes and emperors. He was deadly serious about his vocation, and whatever else may be said about him, he must be given credit for superhuman self-discipline and austerity.

Simeon Stylites (the word *stylites* means pillar) was born in the year 388 in Silicia on the Syrian border, the son of shepherd folk. He apparently had no instruction or education except what he received in church on Sundays. His daily work was caring for the sheep, and Sunday was the great day of his week. He loved the Liturgy, and the instructions impressed him greatly. Out in the fields he tried to imitate what he saw in church. He gathered balsam, for instance, and burned it so that he could offer a "sweet-smelling incense unto the Lord." One winter when he was about thirteen, the snow was too deep to take the sheep out. He could, therefore, get to church oftener, and he learned much more about the Gospel. The day he heard the Beatitudes for the first time he was very much moved. He didn't understand all of the sermon, so he asked an old neighbor to explain. The man told him that prayer, fasting, keeping the night watches, and especially patient suffering were the means of reaching heaven, and he added that a solitary life such as Simeon was leading was best for one who would practice virtue.

Simeon went back to his sheep, but there was a change in his behavior. He fasted a great deal and often spent whole days and nights in the church praying. The other shepherds disapproved of him. The place of a shepherd, they said, was with his sheep, not on his knees in a church. Simeon realized the truth of their criticisms, and he tried his best to correct his faults but without much success. When his father died, he gave his share of the land to his brother, and the money and goods to the poor.

The harvest was early that year, and Simeon decided to gather it just once more on what was now his brother's land. The gleaners, usually women and children, were allowed to follow the reapers and gather whatever sheaves of grain remained on the field. There was a bountiful dinner for the reapers at the end of the day, but the gleaners went unfed. Simeon felt sorry for them and brought out food and drink, but there were many more than he expected and he feared that his supplies would not last. He kept on serving, however, and God multiplied the food miraculously so that the gleaners actually fared better than the reapers. This was Simeon's first miracle.

Simeon now set out to be a monk. He was nearly fifteen and felt that he should delay no longer, so he went to the nearest monastery and asked for admission. Abbot Timothy, who ruled the monastery, rejected Simeon at first because of his age, but the boy remained for days outside the gate without food or drink, begging to be admitted as the lowliest servant. Abbot Timothy at last gave in, and Simeon stayed there for some time. He learned the psalter in less than four months, and in other ways showed himself to have an excellent mind and memory. Moreover he gained the good will of the other monks by his humility and charity.

Two years later he moved on to a larger monastery not far from Antioch. Abbot Heliodorus was a very saintly man who was quite impressed by Simeon's reputation and qualifications. After the young shepherd was admitted, however, the other monks were not so much impressed. They accused him of "singularity." Now singularity is something that is rightly discouraged in any religious community. It is not good for a particular monk or nun to perform excessive penances or in other ways go beyond the rule as if they were trying to establish a reputation for holiness beyond that of their companions.

Abbot Heliodorus watched Simeon. He certainly did seem singular. He trained himself to eat only once a week and to go without sleep. His method of accomplishing that feat was singular enough. He stood on a ball leaning against a wall. When he fell asleep the ball rolled and he fell off. Even when he didn't use the ball, the other monks said that he slept like a bird on a perch. One day the kitchen monk ordered him to stir the fire with a poker which he had previously made red-hot. Simeon did so, but not a mark showed on his hand. When Abbot Heliodorus heard of the incident he was very angry at the kitchen monk, but Simeon interceded for him and he was not punished.

The good abbot was sorely tried by his new monk, however. He realized that the boy was a most unusual and probably a saintly character, but he could not encourage his increasingly unusual behavior. No matter how severe the results of his many mortifications, he refused all remedies. He was discovered, for example, to be wearing around his waist a piece of the tough rope used for the well bucket. It was woven of jagged palm leaves and naturally caused deep wounds which became so infected that it was only with difficulty that his habit could be removed. Even then he refused treatment. When the abbot forbade one practice, Simeon thought of another to replace it.

Simeon spent Lent that year in a deep dark cavern already occupied by poisonous snakes and evil spirits of the kind that plagued most solitaries. His only weapon was the sign of the Cross. One night the cave became suddenly bright and a voice said: "Simeon, thy brethren persecute thee and Satan torments thee, but fear not. The Lord is with thee. His grace will protect thee and His right hand sustain thee. Thou wilt tread Satan under thy feet." Simeon was comforted.

On Easter morning the abbot and some of the monks went out with torches to find him. He returned to the monastery with them and received Communion, but the monks felt little charity in their hearts. They asked Heliodorus to dismiss Simeon because he was a continual source of scandal and anxiety. The good abbot was much distressed, but he finally called Simeon and told him that he would have to leave because his "unauthorized and dangerous singularities" were a stumbling block to the others. Nevertheless, he told the boy that he loved him and wished him well.

"Go where God shall lead thee," he said. "Depart in peace, my son, and God go with you."

Simeon took things as they came. He went out to the desert and lived contentedly in a dry well for some time, but Heliodorus was told in a dream that he had dismissed a very worthy monk. He sent for Simeon, who returned at his bidding but did not stay long. He went next to a lonely hermitage and spent the following Lent in total abstinence, imitating the forty-day fast of Our Lord. A priest friend gave him ten loaves of bread and a goatskin full of water, but when he returned at Easter the bread and water were still there. Simeon appeared to be dead, but when the priest moistened his lips and gave him the Eucharist, he began to recover and was able to eat a few lettuce leaves. After that, he always kept Lent in the same manner, standing upright at first to praise God, then sitting as he grew weaker, and finishing the holy season lying on the ground. Later on, even on his pillar, he kept the same custom. He was a man of rugged constitution and accustomed himself to hardship.

After spending three years at the hermitage Simeon was planning to go out to the desert for good, but his friend and disciple, Daniel, a priest from Antioch, persuaded him that he should maintain contact with the world. Together, they worked out a shelter called a mandra. It was an enclosed space with high walls but open to the weather. In the year 412 at the beginning of Lent, when Simeon was twenty-four years old, he entered the mandra where for nearly fifty years he was to be the teacher and benefactor of thousands of people. Daniel sealed the wall and left him.

On Easter Sunday Daniel came heading a long procession of priests and people. He opened the mandra and gave Communion to Simeon. A man of the neighborhood who had a reputation for great holiness asked Simeon to bless a vessel of oil which he had brought with him. Simeon did so, and immediately the oil overflowed. The people scrambled to put some of it in any container they could find, and when the man took the vessel home it remained miraculously filled, no matter how much he gave away. Many people were thereby cured of their ills.

Soon the blind, the sick, and the crippled began to come from as far away as Spain, France, and Italy to obtain Simeon's blessing. After the Easter miracle the mandra had been kept open, but now Simeon asked to have it closed again, leaving only one small opening through which he could receive Holy Communion. For eighteen months he lived in complete seclusion without nourishment, sometimes standing for whole days and nights in one position.

In the year 423 Simeon began to build his columns. There was a large stone in the mandra about seven feet high. One day he saw a glorious figure standing on it and pointing to him. When Simeon stood on the stone himself, he experienced such a sense of happiness and well-being that he knew God wanted him there for some good reason. He stood on the stone for three months at first. Then he started the first column. During the first seven years he raised the pillar from ten feet high to twenty, to forty, and eventually to eighty. Some historians say that the last column was ninety feet high. His disciples built his columns for him and served him in any way they could.

What does a man do on top of a barren pillar all day and all night? What does he think about? How could Simeon withstand the terrible summer heat and the winter storms? Did he ever look ahead with doubt or fear to endless days and nights without a moment of relief or relaxation? How did he plan his sermons? He had no books, of course—nothing at all except what was in his head.

Simeon wore a rough monk's habit of wool

with a hood and a girdle of rope. In winter he sometimes used a small sheepskin. He had a long, gray beard, and it is said that his face was beautiful and shining with holiness. When his disciples came to supply his few wants, they used a ladder to reach his platform. Sometimes they brought a few dried lentils, or a little water, or perhaps a new garment when the old one would no longer hold together. He preached twice a day, and on Sundays and holydays he remained all day and all night with his hands raised in prayer to God. He suffered a great deal from ulcers on his spine and on his feet, but he did nothing to prevent or cure them.

As might be expected, Simeon had many severe critics. They disliked his singularity and considered his behavior merely sensational with nothing of holiness about it. The monks at Tabenna were scandalized at first, but they finally accepted him. Once the bishops decided to test his humility by ordering him to come down. He obediently made ready to do so, but when they found that they could not shake his obedience or humility, they gave up and told him to stay where he was.

Standing there on his pillar, Simeon Stylites saw all the miseries of the world in terrible array. He stood there while Vandals, Goths, and Huns rolled over the Roman empire. He saw great heresies arise and did his part in fighting them. All kinds of people came to consult him, from the gentle Emperor Theodosius II to the frightened survivors of the disastrous earthquake that laid Antioch in ruins, who came weeping to camp around his pillar which had miraculously remained erect.

Not long afterward Simeon realized that he was nearing his end. His favorite disciple, Antony, remained constantly near by. The patriarch of Antioch came and administered the Sacraments. For three days Simeon lay unconscious while clouds of sweet-smelling incense from an unseen source surrounded the pillar and the people knelt and prayed. At last when Simeon seemed trying to rouse himself, Antony climbed the ladder to hear the last words of his master. Simeon bowed three times and looked up to heaven. He blessed all four quarters of the world with his hand and spoke a few last words of love and blessing to his disciples. Then he rested his tired head on Antony's shoulder and died.

The emperor wanted Simeon's body brought to Constantinople as a holy treasure, but the people of Antioch raised such great lamentation that the emperor yielded. He permitted them to build a chapel amid the ruins of Antioch, and the mandra where Simeon had lived so long and the pillar on which he stood became a place of pilgrimage.

So ended the life of one of God's most unusual saints. His whole life was, in a sense, a miracle, and he was considered one of the wonders of the century in which he lived. He still remains a miracle to those who read of him today, and as we read we wonder if some such example of humility, steadfastness, and stern self-discipline is not badly needed in our own troubled times.

CHAPTER THIRTEEN

St. Cyril of Alexandria

We are inclined to think of the saints as gentle, lovable persons who spent most of their time fasting and praying and carrying baskets of food to the poor. As a matter of fact, some of them had decidedly unpleasant traits. There was St. Cyril of Alexandria, for example. He was proud, obstinate, jealous, and domineering. He was ill-mannered, impulsive, and frequently unjust. He had no patience and little diplomacy, and he hung onto grudges. Nobody has a good word to say for his personality, but what a mind the man had! With what uncompromising courage he fought heresy! Cyril needed all his toughness to defend the honor of God's holy Mother; and just as we remember St. Athanasius when we say the Nicene Creed, we must also give credit to stubborn, fighting Cyril of Alexandria when we say in the litany, "*Sancta Dei Genetrix*," or when we conclude the Hail Mary with "Holy Mary, Mother of God, pray for us."

Cyril came from an important Greek family and was educated in the famous schools of Alexandria where he learned to dislike and distrust the people of Antioch and to despise their methods of education. His uncle, Theophilus of Alexandria, was the bitter enemy of St. John Chrysostom, patriarch of Antioch, and Cyril unnecessarily carried on the feud. Some of Cyril's least worthy characteristics could well be traced to his uncle. He was of a lordly and imposing appearance with a trace of arrogance in his manner. He could command respect but not affection. When Theophilus died in the year 412, Cyril succeeded him as patriarch of Alexandria. Almost immediately he came into conflict with Orestes, the governor of the city, because of certain justifiable but undiplomatic acts, and the feud between them had serious consequences.

There lived in Alexandria at that time a remarkable woman named Hypatia. She was the brilliant daughter of a learned pagan philosopher and taught philosophy herself to crowds of students. She had so much self-confidence and such an air of authority that she was the greatest pagan influence in the city. Moreover she was much respected and often consulted by the governor. Now Orestes had no liking for Cyril and his domineering methods. He was well aware that the patriarch had more influence in the city than he himself.

It happened that there was in Alexandria just then a large and unruly segment of the population that needed very little encouragement to become a mob. It comprised chiefly a number of tough, sturdy men who had served the city in time of plague when others fled in fear. They were lawless, violent, and acted on impulse, and a great many of them, unhappily, were Christians. When they heard that Hypatia had influenced Orestes against Cyril, they didn't stop to ask any questions. They waited for her chariot, dragged her out of it, and literally tore her to pieces. Then they burned what remained of her body. This terrible outrage put both Cyril and the Christians of Alexandria in a very unfortunate situation. Cyril was quite honestly sorry and ashamed, but the governor declared him to be the instigator of the crime and ordered him banished from the city.

The Christians naturally defended their patriarch, but even the pagans pointed out that Cyril was the only one who could control the disorderly elements and prevent further trouble. Orestes reluctantly rescinded his order of exile, but the feeling on both sides was intense. By this time the number of monks had grown tremendously and, whereas they had originally lived chiefly in the deserts, there were now many monasteries to be found in the large cities. The monks, in general, performed a great service and courageously supported every movement against heresy, but as had always been the case, there were a few troublemakers among them. One day a small group of monks insulted the governor on the street and actually wounded him slightly. Thereupon Orestes had one of the monks seized and tortured. Cyril then, throwing caution to the winds, had the monk's body brought into the church where he preached a powerful panegyric declaring the man to be a martyr. Not even the Christians agreed with Cyril in this case, and the act did nothing to heal the breach, but a still greater battle was already beginning to take shape.

The current patriarch of Constantinople, whose name was Nestorius, had once been a monk in a laura near Antioch. After his ordination he established quite a reputation as a preacher and was regarded by the people as another John Chrysostom. As he grew more assured, however, there were murmurings that he was a firebrand and that nothing but trouble would come of his unbridled tongue. By this time, early in the fifth century, Arianism had nearly disappeared. All Catholics believed that Christ the Son is equal to and consubstantial with the Father and that He had a perfect human nature, complete with body and soul.

Now Nestorius began to preach a new heresy. He taught that Christ was a whole and perfect man, but that He was not actually God. He asserted that the Spirit of God came down and dwelt in Christ much as the Spirit of God had dwelt in the prophets. He declared, moreover, that Christ was really two persons, a divine person dwelling in a human person. Now the Catholic faith is that Christ is one Person with two natures, the nature of God and the nature of man; that He is really and completely God and really and completely man, yet completely and inseparably one. He is both God and man. This Nestorius denied. He declared that the Godhood dwelt in the manhood as in a temple.

The next step in the Nestorian heresy was to deny the Incarnation and to assert that Mary was not the Mother of God. She was the mother of Christ, said the Nestorians, but not the Mother of God. She was the mother only of His human nature. The Nestorian heresy spread from Constantinople all over the East and, as is usual with heresies, caused great dissension in the Church. Nestorian bishops excommunicated all who used the title, Mother of God. But a fearless champion arose to defend the Blessed Virgin's honor, and that was Cyril of Alexandria.

Cyril first sent a mild protest to Nestorius and received a contemptuous answer. Then he sent out a Paschal letter warning against the heresy and defending Mary's title as Mother of God. Nestorius angrily alleged interference, although Cyril had merely addressed his own people in Alexandria. Now, however, he came out boldly and charged Nestorius with heresy, and the battle began. More than heresy was involved, however. Alexandria was the first see in the East and ranked second to Rome. Constantinople wanted that spot. The bitter rivalry went on from time to time for more than two hundred years and the Nestorian conflict was only one of the high points, but it finally involved the whole Eastern Church, and the

Emperor, Theodosius II, was obliged to interfere. Eventually both sides appealed to Pope Celestine.

The Pope was holding a synod in Rome in the year 430, and Cyril sent one of his deacons with a complete account of the whole controversy. Pope Celestine gave entire approval to Cyril's side of the argument and ordered Nestorius to retract the heresy in writing within ten days or be excommunicated. The Pope appointed Cyril as his deputy to carry out the sentence. That appointment, naturally, aroused Nestorius still further. He absolutely refused to sign the retraction and hurled insults at "that Egyptian," meaning Cyril.

At last the emperor called a general council to be held at Ephesus at Whitsuntide of the year 431. The ancient Greek city of Ephesus (near what is now the site of the city of Smyrna in Turkey) was famous for many reasons. It was a very beautiful city, with its buildings of gleaming marble and its fine harbor where the shipping of the world rode at anchor. In Ephesus the pagans worshiped the goddess Diana and made the city ring with the cry: "Great is Diana of the Ephesians!" It was to Ephesus that St. Paul went on one of his missionary journeys and to Ephesus that he sent his "Epistles to the Ephesians." St.

John the Evangelist was the first bishop of Ephesus, and according to tradition, the Blessed Virgin lived there for some time. But the greatest glory of that city was that the Council of Ephesus, in the year 431, established Mary's title of *Theotokos*, God-bearer, Mother of God.

Two hundred bishops gathered in Ephesus on the twenty-first of June, together with priests and deacons, scribes and secretaries, with Cyril of Alexandria presiding as senior patriarch and representative of the Pope, and an imperial commission sent by Theodosius. Cyril brought with him fifty Egyptian bishops, and he had the weight of both Pope and emperor on his side. The council took place in the Church of Our Lady and St. John, known as the double church because of its curious architecture.

When the council began, Nestorius did not appear. He had expected his friend, John of Antioch, to be present, but the archbishop had not arrived. The council waited for several days but at last began its deliberations without him. The bishops condemned the Nestorian heresies and affirmed the title of Mary as *Theotokos*, or Mother of God. Nestorius was offically deposed and excommunicated. Then the council proceeded to other matters.

Six days later John of Antioch arrived with

forty-one Syrian bishops. They refused to join the council called by the emperor and convened a separate synod during which they excommunicated on false charges Cyril and all those who were attending the official council. That council then reported to the emperor that they had acted correctly and canonically under the authority of the Pope. They invited John of Antioch once again to the council and, when he refused, they imposed excommunication upon him and declared the excommunication of Cyril null and void.

That wasn't the end of the matter, however. The emperor finally decided to punish everyone concerned. He deposed John, Nestorius, and Cyril and imprisoned both Cyril and Nestorius, but neither side was satisfied. Then the emperor went over all the evidence again and finally decided that Cyril was right. Cyril was allowed to return to Alexandria, where he was received with honor and hailed as a second Athanasius. John of Antioch returned to his own see and apparently thought things over. He eventually made peace with Cyril, condemned Nestorius, and made a clear statement of his own faith.

It is hard for us now to understand these violent arguments and quarrels that so often threatened the unity of the early Church, particularly in the East, but it is easy enough to see how they could happen. All of the leading figures of that time, both pagans and Christians, were trained in the Greek tradition. They were thinkers, debaters, and orators, fluent and eloquent. Their tongues were their swords. But the various "schools" or centers of learning, while following the same general pattern of studies, showed very different characteristics in their ways of thinking and of stating their conclusions. Alexandria and Antioch were especially far apart, the Alexandrian idealism always being at odds with the realistic, literal-mindedness of Antioch. What seemed truth to one side, might sound like heresy to the other, especially since the principal cities were rivals, not only in religious matters, but in nearly everything else. They just found it hard to agree on anything, but such men of powerful intellect and wisdom as Athanasius, Basil, John Chrysostom, and Cyril of Alexandria discovered every flaw in logic. They could not be deceived by words, and out of the bitter quarrels and heresies came clear, exact statements of the Christian faith.

Some historians have said that had Cyril of Alexandria been more of a diplomat he might have avoided some of the trouble between

Alexandria and Antioch and perhaps even have prevented the rise of Nestorianism. However that may be, when a strong, firm voice was needed to defend the true meaning of some point of Christian belief, Cyril's voice was raised. He was the last of the remarkable group of Fathers that began with Athanasius, and for his sound and systematic theology, he ranks in the Eastern Church with Aquinas in the West.

Cyril of Alexandria died in the year 444. He was never greatly loved, but he was admired and respected even by those who disliked him. He was sometimes criticized for not using purer Greek in his writing and for not cultivating a clearer style, but he considered style of little importance. He cared nothing for eloquence or persuasive oratory. All he wanted was the truth in plain, unadorned language that could not be misunderstood, and as time went on his true worth came to be appreciated much more than in his own day.

In 1882, Pope Leo XIII made St. Cyril a Doctor of the Church, and in 1944, Pope Pius XII, in an encyclical on the Eastern Church, called him "the light of Christian wisdom and a valiant hero of the apostolate." And it is because of Cyril's valiant defense of the Blessed Virgin's honor that the Eastern liturgy still retains its prayer:

Mother of God, Theotokos,
Mother of Christ, Khristotokos,
Mother of eternal love,
Mother of Divine Grace,
Rejoice, hail and save those who have hope in thee.

CHAPTER FOURTEEN

St. John Damascene

St. John Damascene is regarded as the last of the Greek Fathers, though he was born more than three hundred years after Cyril of Alexandria, in a far different age and in a strange environment—and his story sounds like a tale from the *Arabian Nights*. John was born in the fabulous city of Damascus and lived out his life under the protection of Moslem rulers. His father, a man of wealth and influence, was the caliph's vizier, holding a position of trust in the Mohammedan government. John eventually succeeded his father, although the life did not suit him. He wanted to be a simple monk in a quiet monastery, and he finally achieved his goal though certainly not as he had planned it. He became a famous poet and a learned theologian; and from his Moslem stronghold, using his voice and pen as weapons, he waged battle against the Christian emperors and the heresy of iconoclasm which forbade the use of pictures or images for religious purposes.

The ancient city of Damascus is said to have been founded by a great-grandson of Noah. It was a great and flourishing seaport when Solomon ruled over Jerusalem. Seventeen centuries before Christ was born, the beautiful city was ruled by Egyptians and later, in turn, by Assyrians, Chaldeans, Persians, Macedonians, Romans, and Arabs. Known as the Queen City of the East, it commanded the highways of western Asia. Ships from all over the world came into its blue harbor, and caravans carried the colorful cargoes to Baghdad, Mecca, Stambul, and other centers of commerce. It was on the road to Damascus that Saul of Tarsus was stricken blind. It was to a house in the Street called Straight that God sent Ananias to find Saul and baptize him and change him to Paul. And it was from the city of Damascus that St. John Damascene takes his name.

For many centuries Damascus was a Christian city, second only to Antioch, but by the time John Damascene came into the world, near the end of the seventh century, it had become the center of the Mohammedan kingdom, a city of white minarets and golden domes set amid rich green foliage. The caliphs, or rulers, were usually just and liberal to the Christians, allowing them to hold public office, to engage in business or the arts, and to keep a number of their churches open. There were usually many Christians holding high positions at court.

The father of John Damascene was a Christian of Greek descent, usually called by the Arabic name Mansur. He owned vast properties in Judea and Palestine, and, being charitable as well as rich, one of his chief interests was redeeming Christian captives. His son John, born sometime between 680 and 690, was the apple of his eye and his education a matter of great concern.

Most boys of that time were taught to ride, to use various weapons, to hunt, and to take part in athletic contests, but John Mansur had other ideas. He had no intention of educating his son to violence and cruelty. The boy's tutors were instructed to develop his mind and soul with all diligence, rather than his body. A fortunate circumstance put the boy into the hands of a remarkable teacher. After a certain raid on the coast of Sicily, John Mansur ransomed a number of slaves among whom was a Greek monk named Cosmas, a man of extraordinary intellect. A priest as well as a monk, he was highly skilled in grammar, rhetoric, and logic, to say nothing of music, poetry, astronomy, arithmetic, and geometry. John Mansur had to pay a very high ransom for Cosmas, but he was well repaid. There was a second boy in the household, an adopted brother of young John who was also named Cosmas, and the two boys studied together. Both John and Cosmas were excellent students and they were well trained in all the virtues, as well as skills, by their priest tutor.

Much of John's training, of course, was directed toward his expected career in government office. When his father died he was prepared to take his place and, assuming in his turn the name of John Mansur, he served competently under several caliphs. The Moslem rulers never interfered with the religion of their Christian officers, and John had no difficulty on that score. He and his adopted brother were both interested in writing, especially poetry, and John wrote widely on Christian themes, including many fiery treatises against the spreading heresy of iconoclasm. But neither of the young men liked public life. They decided to become monks.

Having made their decision and set their worldly affairs in order, John and Cosmas set out for the laura of St. Sabas, called Mar Saba, near Jerusalem. Mar Saba was a very old and picturesque monastery with its copper dome rising dramatically out of the rocks on the road to Jericho. It was built like a fortress with thick walls, towers, and gates, and with many balconies and bridges crossing deep chasms. The place just suited John and Cosmas, who settled quickly into the routine of a monk's life—but with a difference. They both continued to write poems and hymns. They wrote the music, too, and enjoyed singing their own compositions. These unusual activities did not please the older monks. They branded the two novices as disturbing elements. When John, at the request of another monk, wrote a hymn on death and set it to joyous music, the venerable monk who was his cell-mate and instructor was outraged. He believed that death was a time for mourning and weeping, not for singing and joy, and he ordered John out of their cell. The old man had a vision later that changed his mind, and he told John to come back and write whatever he liked. Gratefully, John resumed his writing, and his poems, as well as those of Cosmas, became very famous.

The patriarch of Jerusalem was much interested in these two gifted young men and thought that their talents should not be buried in a monastery. He ordained Cosmas, much against his will, to be bishop of the port city of Gaza. Then he made John a priest and moved him to Jerusalem where for a while he preached and wrote brilliant arguments against the heretics. Cosmas resigned himself and became a very good bishop, but John could not be contented in Jerusalem. Eventually, he went back to Mar Saba and spent the rest of his days in studying, writing, collecting and arranging old manuscripts, and revising all his own work, pruning it, as he said, of all his youthful "blossoms of rhetoric."

Iconoclasm was the last of the great heresies that arose in the Eastern Church. It lasted altogether over a hundred years and spanned the reigns of many popes and emperors in waves of argument and persecution. The word *iconoclast* means a breaker of ikons, or images, and therefore, one who opposes the use of pictures or images in church worship. Christians had made use of pictures from the earliest days. As the years went on, the images became more elaborate and beautiful. In the West, statues of wood or marble were commonly used, whereas the artists of the East were more inclined to flat paintings and mosaics. The cross was a frequently used symbol. After a time, the figure of Christ was added and the cross became a crucifix. In the East, a picture of Christ enthroned and surrounded by saints was very popular. Christians never adored these images. They respected them as reminders of sacred persons and as a means of paying tribute to God.

The heresy of iconoclasm was an unusual one in that it involved so seemingly small and unimportant a matter. Most of the great controversies in the Church had concerned difficult questions of theology that interested scholars, chiefly, and religious leaders. The common people did not understand or care very much, but when the emperor's troops dared to enter the churches and tear down the sacred ikons, they understood only too well and they felt very strongly about it. The clergy were indignant, too, because the government was interfering in a purely religious matter, whereas the bishops had consistently declared that the government had no right to make laws for the Church.

The Moslem religion does not permit pictures of any living thing, even on stamps or coins. The Christians, therefore, in this eighth-century outbreak of persecution, believed that the trouble was probably started by Moslems, but some Christians began to say that it was a good idea to ban all images since they offended both Jews and Moslems. The Mohammedan governor naturally supported these groups, and a major persecution was soon under way. A number of successive emperors made laws forbidding the use of all pictures and statues. Emperor Leo III ordered all ikons to be destroyed and forbade anyone to keep them or honor them. He even went so far as to write to Pope Gregory and order him to destroy all such images in Rome—or expect the emperor's soldiers to attend to it!

Pope Gregory answered calmly, expressing his surprise that the emperor did not know the difference between a statue and an idol. Leo's reply was greater violence and even stricter laws, whereupon Pope Gregory excommunicated him. Constantine V carried on the war relentlessly. He burned and destroyed a number of lauras, and many a monk died a martyr. When Emperor Leo IV came to power he eased up on the restrictions, and after his death his wife Irene, who became regent for her son Constantine VI, followed his example. The people breathed freely again and cautiously restored their ikons.

In the year 787, the Second Council of Nicaea was called. It was the seventh ecumenical council and was attended by three hundred bishops. Among other important matters, the council made very clear the difference between honoring images and adoring them. The last session of the council was held in Constantinople in the presence of Empress Irene and her son, and the persecutions died down. It was not, however, until the reign of Empress Theodora, regent for her son Michael III, that peace was finally restored. The ikons were returned to the cathedral of the Holy Wisdom in Constantinople in a solemn procession on the first Sunday of Lent. That same feast of rejoicing, known as the Feast of Orthodoxy, is still celebrated in the Byzantine Church. The word *orthodox* at first applied only to the matter of the ikons, but after the Great Schism in 1054 it was assumed as a title by those Eastern churches which withdrew from the Church Universal and refused to accept the Pope as the true successor of Christ.

During the persecutions of the early eighth century, the patriarchs of the Eastern Church wavered back and forth on the question of images, sometimes making determined opposition, but often deferring to the emperor's commands. But the Pope of Rome never swerved from his position, and he was supported in the

East by the valiant and eloquent pen of John Damascene, who became the chief defender of the faith. It was immediately after Emperor Leo III published his first edict against the ikons that John wrote his famous treatise entitled "Against the Destroyer of Holy Ikons," and he continued to write and preach and stir the people to resistance until his death at Mar Saba in 754. Furious emperors yearned to get their hands upon John, but he never crossed the frontier into the Roman Empire and he presented the strange spectacle of a Christian protected from Christian emperors by Moslem caliphs. John did not live to see the final triumph against the Iconoclasts, but his tongue and his pen did much to bring it about.

In spite of all his solid scholarship, it was poetry that John loved best, and one of his finest compositions is the dramatic Paschal Ode sung in the Byzantine Church at Easter. At the stroke of midnight after the Easter vigil, the chief priest lifts up the cross in the darkness and cries out, "Christ is risen!" Immediately the cry is repeated by the people. The candles flare into glory and out rolls the music of St. John's magnificent Resurrection canon: "Christ is risen from the dead!" He must sometimes lean from the wall of heaven to listen once again.

The work of St. John Damascene was not all original. He made a great contribution to successive generations by his work of compiling and arranging the writings of the earlier Greek Fathers. He had great respect for science and so great a reputation in philosophy, logic, and psychology that many of his writings are still standard works in the Eastern Church.

St. John Damascene was declared a Doctor of the Church by Pope Leo XIII in 1890, and in the collect of his Mass on March 27 we pray:

Almighty and eternal God who didst give to blessed John heavenly knowledge and admirable strength of mind to defend the worship of holy images: grant by his prayers and example that we may copy the virtues and enjoy the protection of those whose pictures we honor.

CHAPTER FIFTEEN

Mount Athos

The most famous spiritual center of Orthodox Christianity is Mount Athos near Thessalonica in northern Greece. It is not a single monastery, as one might suppose, but a small republic comprising twenty separate and widely differentiated monasteries sprawling the length of a rugged mountainous peninsula thirty-five miles long. Thomas Merton calls it the "last important Christian survival of the typical ancient monastic colonies which flourished in the fourth and fifth centuries." If in God's good time Mount Athos, the Holy Mountain, should return to the Church of Rome, the line of Catholic monasticism would be unbroken from St. Paul the Hermit and St. Antony of Egypt until the present day.

On Mount Athos can be found a great variety of monks and monasteries, some of austere and strict observance, others of a more liberal trend, and the liturgy is chanted in many forms and languages. The monks are poor. They earn their living not by weaving mats and baskets, but chiefly by cutting timber and making wine or olive oil. Out on the steep hillsides dwell the hermits and solitaries in their lonely caves and cells, fasting, praying, and sleeping on the bare ground in their rude and comfortless shelters just as they did in the Egyptian and Syrian deserts long ago. One of the most interesting groups is the Russian colony, once a flourishing and powerful unit but now greatly reduced in numbers, as are those of Serbia, Bulgaria, and Rumania, since vocations from the Iron Curtain countries are practically nonexistent and only very old monks remain.

By the ninth century the Church was well established in most of Western Europe, but the more eastern provinces were still pagan.

Some missionary work had been done in that territory by two brothers named Cyril and Methodius, and when an ambassador from Moravia came to Constantinople to ask for missionaries who could speak the Slavonic language, Emperor Michael III thought at once of the two young monks. Mount Athos was not founded until nearly a century later, but it was from Thessalonica that Cyril and Methodius set out in 862 and made their way up the Danube River to Moravia on their difficult mission.

The first thing necessary in order to reach the people was an alphabet and a written language. Cyril set to work on this problem and, assisted by Methodius, compiled a set of characters based on the Greek letters. Then he organized and stabilized the Slavonic tongue and wrote a grammar. So scholarly and efficient was his work that it became the basis for all Slavic languages, and the "Cyrillic alphabet" is used today by Russians, Serbs, and Bulgarians.

After they had a written language, the next step for Cyril and Methodius was to secure permission to use it in the liturgy. There was much opposition by churchmen to such innovations, but when the brothers went to Rome and stated their case to Pope Adrian II he agreed with them. He also decreed that they should both be raised to the rank of bishop with the power of ordaining their own priests and deacons. Methodius did become a bishop, but it is not certain that Cyril lived to be consecrated. He died there in Rome in 869, far from the scene of his monumental work, and Methodius went sadly to the Pope. His mother's last wish had been that if either son should die, the other would bring his body back home for burial. Methodius wished to leave at once.

Pope Adrian was sympathetic, but he argued that so distinguished a man should be buried in Rome and that his mother would be satisfied and honored. So Cyril was buried with great ceremony in the Church of San Clemente, and Methodius, who was called by the Pope "a man of exact understanding and orthodoxy," returned to Moravia as papal legate and metropolitan of a large area extending to the borders of Bulgaria. He had constant trouble with neighboring German bishops and spent two years imprisoned by them in a leaky cell. Pope John VIII finally got him out, but he withdrew the privilege of using Slavonic in the liturgy.

Methodius remained at his post, the object of petty persecution, but in the end he persuaded Pope John to change his mind. "God Who made the three principal languages, Hebrew, Greek, and Latin," said the Pope at last, "made others also for His honor and glory." And when Methodius died in 884, his funeral service was conducted in Greek, Slavonic, and Latin. He was dearly loved by the Slavs for all that he and Cyril had done for them, and both are still venerated by Catholic Czechs, Slovaks, and Croats, and by Orthodox Serbs and Bulgars. In 1880, Pope Leo XIII made Methodius the patron of church unity and of all works devoted to the return of the separated Slavs to the Church of Rome.

During the late ninth century, largely due to the groundwork of Cyril and Methodius, large groups of Bulgars, Moravians, Bohemians, Ruthenians, Hungarians, and Poles came into the Christian Church. It was in the year 945 that Princess Olga of Kiev, in the Ukraine, became a Christian. Later, through her grandson, she was instrumental in converting all the Ukrainian people. Olga was a woman of peasant stock, shrewd and clever, and before her conversion had been cruel and barbarous, as were many of the northern peoples. When her husband, Prince Igor, was assassinated, she had his murderers scalded to death with white-hot steam and thousands of their followers slain.

Shortly after Prince Igor's death, Olga, then acting as regent for her son, was converted and baptized, probably in Constantinople. She became a very able administrator, ruled the state wisely, and introduced many Christian practices. She built churches in Kiev and in her own home village, erected wayside crosses, and gave generously to the poor. She wrote to the German emperor, Otto the Great, asking him to send missionaries to her country. He did so but the mission was unsuccessful because, unlike Cyril and Methodius, the missionaries did not use the Slavonic language. Olga died in 969 at a very great age, and, although Russia as we know it today did not then exist, she is popularly regarded as one of the first Russian-born Christians.

It was in 988 that Olga's grandson, the brutal, bloodthirsty pagan Vladimer, was married to a Greek princess and converted to Christianity, and the conversion of the Kiev Ruthenians or Russians dates from that time. Vladimer had all the pagan idols destroyed and sent for Greek clergy of the Byzantine Rite to establish the Church. By now there were monasteries all over the Byzantine empire, the foundations of the great monastery of Mount Athos were just being laid, and a small boy named Antony was studying with his tutors in Kiev and dreaming of becoming a monk. When he grew up and had finished his education, he did become a monk. He made a pilgrimage to Mount Athos, which was by that time well established, and there he would gladly have remained. His abbot, however, insisted that he go back to his own land where he was needed.

When Antony returned to Kiev, he wanted to start a monastery something like Mount Athos, but he had nothing with which to build. Instead, he went to live in a mountainous region where there were many caves, and there came to him disciples who, under his direction, "with tears and fasting and prayer" built a monastery. They built a church in one large cave and a refectory in another, but even after they were able to erect other buildings the monastery was still known as the Caves of Kiev.

About 1032, there came to the Caves a young monk named Theodosius, intelligent, learned, and confident. Antony, still a hermit at heart and recognizing the gift of leadership in Theodosius, placed the monastery under his direction. Theodosius put the community under strict discipline. He built a hostel for travelers, a hospital, and an orphanage, and sent out monks to the city to perform the corporal works of mercy. Antony still loved the tradition of the early Egyptian monks and took for his model his namesake, the first St. Antony, but Theodosius preferred the pattern of the monks of Palestine. He could understand

Antony's longing for solitude, but it was his own belief that a "Lord have mercy on us" prayed from the heart collectively by the community was of greater spiritual value than the whole psalter recited by one monk in his cell. Under his leadership the Caves of Kiev became a great influence throughout the country.

St. Antony died in his own old cave in 1073 at the age of ninety, and St. Theodosius died only a year later. As years went by the monastery was many times destroyed by Tartars, but always it was restored and it survived until the beginning of the Bolshevist regime in Russia about 1914. Antony and Theodosius died nearly twenty years after the final break between the Eastern Church and Rome, but their feasts are kept by Catholic Russians and Ruthenians as well as by the Orthodox Churches.

So there is a long line extending from the first St. Antony in the Egyptian desert to St. Antony of the Caves of Kiev, who was himself a monk at Mount Athos. Today, a thousand years later, Mount Athos still stands, a center of Orthodox faith, aloof and separated from Rome. And now Pope John XXIII is calling the twentieth ecumenical council to discuss the problems facing the Church today and to advance if possible the hope of a united

Church—one Lord, one faith, one baptism. It may not come in our day, but come it must; and to that end all the Catholics of the world are praying.

PRAYER COMPOSED BY A RUSSIAN CATHOLIC PRIEST

Hear, Lord Jesus, the prayers of your unworthy, sinful servants who humbly call upon you. Make us to be one in your One, Holy, Apostolic Church; flood our souls with your unquenchable light; put an end to religious disagreements, that we may all worship you with a single heart and voice. Fulfill quickly, grace-giving Lord, your promise that there shall be one flock and one shepherd. May all men recognize your one Church, and may we be made worthy to glorify your holy name now and forever, world without end. Amen.

Saints of the Byzantine World

	DATE OF BIRTH – DATE OF DEATH	FEAST DAY
St. Paul the Hermit	?–341	January 15
St. Antony of Egypt	251–356	January 17
St. Hilarion	292–371	October 21
St. Pachomius	?–348	May 14
St. Athanasius	293–373	May 2
St. Basil the Great	329–379	June 14
St. Gregory Nazianzen	330–390	May 9
St. Gregory of Nyssa	331?–394?	March 9
St. Macrina	?–379	July 19
St. Cyril of Jerusalem	315–386	March 18
St. John Chrysostom	344–407	January 27
St. Nicholas of Myra	?–?	December 6
St. Simeon Stylites	388–459	January 5
St. Cyril of Alexandria	376–444	January 28
St. John Damascene	680?–754	March 27
St. Cyril	826?–869	July 7
St. Methodius	815?–884	July 7
St. Antony	983–1073	July 10
St. Theodosius	?–1074	May 3
St. Olga	?–969	July 11